D0207332

LINCOLN BEACHEY
The Man Who Owned the Sky

WITHDRAWN
Damaged, Obsolete, or Surplus
Jackson County Library Services

DAMAGE NOTED

Lincoln Beachey is prepared for take-off at the Iowa State Fair, 1914.
This picture, made into a postcard, sold more than a million copies.

Warren Eaton, left, was Beachey's assistant; Art Mix, right, is ready to
spin the propeller, which faced the back of the plane (a "pusher").

IMAGE NOIR

LINCOLN BEACHEY
The Man Who Owned the Sky

Frank Marrero

Tripod Press
Marin County, California
2017

This book, like my whole life, is dedicated to Avatar Adi Da Samraj, Whom I am graced to call "Beloved".

Book and cover design: Brad Reynolds
Original Editor: Susan Little
Second Edition

Copyright © 1997, 2017 Frank Marrero

Tripod Press
Marin County, California

No part of this book may be reproduced in any form or by any electronic or mechanical means, including information storage and retrieval systems, without permission in writing from the publisher, except by a reviewer, who may quote brief passages.

ISBN 978-0-9673265-3-5

Acknowledgments

Gratitude belongs to Jim Heig and Susan Little, for molding my original story into legible form.

Special thanks are due also to Hud Weeks and his son Cooper for their personal collection of photographs and historical documentation on the life of Lincoln Beachey.

Praise to the the museums, curators, archivists, and librarians who helped with the research:

The San Diego National Historical Aerospace Museum
Ray Wagner and Ed Leisner, Archivists.
The Glenn Curtiss Museum, Hammondsport / New York
Lindsley A. Dunn, Curator
The Smithsonian National Air and Space Museum / Washington, D.C.
Paul Garber, Historian Emeritus
The Early Birds of Aviation Inc. / Orange, California
Early Birds: Glenn Messer, Forest Wysong, P.H. Spencer.
The Dominguez Historic Museum / Los Angeles, California
Father Patrick McPolin, Curator.
Columbia University Oral History Department / New York, New York
City of Hammondsport, Archives / Hammondsport, New York
City of Chicago, Archives/ Chicago, Illinois
City of Portland, Archives / Portland, Oregon
City of San Francisco, Archives / San Francisco, California
City of San Diego, Archives / San Diego, California
City of Oakland, Archives / Oakland, California
City of Niagara Falls, Archives / Niagara Falls, Canada
City of Niagara Falls, Archives / Niagara Falls, New York
City of Nashville, Archives / Nashville, Tennessee
City of Washington D.C., Archives
The Nut Tree Restaurant / Vacaville, California

Dearest appreciations go to the following attendants of the 1915 World's Fair for their enthusiastic memories:

Annabel Cornado

Sam Knowles

James O'Brian

Bert Van Cleve

Jack Downey

James Downey

Tom Proctor

Mrs. Gordon Ramsey

Eleanor Jones

Angello Del'Rea

Jeanne Williams

Special thanks to the following:

The Early Birds / This is a club of pilots who soloed before WWI and who were kind enough to let me be an Early Birds Associate. Extra thanks go to Forest Wysong for his extensive interviews. Wysong flew as an aviator with Beachey at Chicago, 1911. Eleven years later, he "soloed" Charles Lindberg.

Bill Robie / Early aviation historian;

Vern Dalhman / Aerobatic Pilot/Beachey Re-creator;

Johnny Van Pelt / Spectator at the 1910 Los Angeles Air Meet;

Gary Lanthrum / Aerobatic pilot, friend, fool, genius, contributing editor;

Grateful thanks to friend and fellow devotee Brad Reynolds for his creative support and superb layout of this book;

Special thanks to the Hiller Aviation Museum who keeps the repository of The Lincoln Beachey Collection. Any pictures NOT credited in this text are from this Collection.

Deepest thanks goes to Adi Da Eleutherios / Beloved Friend who showed me how to write, to breathe, to discern, to meditate, to give, and to love without ceasing.

Table of Contents

The author flies behind a car in Tennessee, 1969.
(Hang gliding officially began in 1972.)

The real Lincoln Beachey
looking up to the sky.

As a senior in high school, the author
dressed as Lincoln Beachey once a week.

Author's Note

E ven as a small child, I was devoted to the flying feeling—which expressed itself in many ways. When I was but two years of age in 1954, I was in the newspapers and on television going off the high dive. I progressed over the years into vaulting from giant waterfalls and precipitous cliffs in the mountains of Tennessee. Starting at ten, I worked daily on developing rope-swinging as an art, dancing and spinning from tree to tree in the woods behind my house. It was a daily Backyard du Soleil, which strengthened for years. Also at ten years of age, I became passionate about Tchaikovsky's soaring first violin concerto and Beethoven's floating and rushing sonatas. Soon thereafter, I dreamed I was piloting a one-man dirigible. I began to fly ecstatically in my dreams, which continues to this day. Beginning in the middle grades, I began to read everything I could about the beginning of flight. When we would travel, I would find the nearest library and rush to the call number: 629.13, aviation history. The story of Lincoln Beachey was of particular interest because I also regularly did feats that required a serious perfection. In my flying-rope art, I would drop multiple stories with a knotted cord in my hands, jerking at last inches from disaster to go on spinning and flying. Borrowing Beachey's own terminology, I named this feat, "The Dive of Death."

When I was sixteen in 1968, my best friend, Gary Lanthrum, and I drove five hundred miles to the Rockford, Illinois Experimental Aircraft Association Fly-In to see a Curtiss Pusher, the kind Beachey piloted. There, I had my first flight—in a 1936 Ford Tri-motor. When Gary and I returned, we built our own flying machine, a crude glider. Crude is actually an understatement. But to Gary and me, it was impressive. Some guy in California was jumping off the sand dunes in one and managed to glide briefly. We wrote him and he sent back a one-page sketch, at the bottom of which was written, "Do not sue Richard

Miller". OK. We built a Rogallo wing out of 16' bamboo sticks and 4 mil plastic drop-cloth from the family hardware store in Nashville. We hinged the bamboo with gate hinges, and the plastic was attached with duct tape: it worked great, as we were able to take giant steps as we ran down steep streets near our house. As far as we can tell, Gary and I were the first people to hang-glide outside of California. These Richard Miller "bamboo butterflies" were the great granddaddies of today's hang gliders, a sport that officially began in 1972.

Gary's family moved to Portland, Oregon where Gary built another "bamboo-butterfly" and ran down some hills outside of Portland, trying to get airborne. The farmer whose land he was trespassing on came along and offered to pull Gary with a light-weight rope and his tractor. But he couldn't get going fast enough. So the farmer went back to his house and got his car. (Ah, the old days…) Gary called me that night and told me the good news: the car and the rope worked, he had flown! I went immediately to the hardware store, bought supplies, and that weekend tied myself to a car with 150 feet of parachute chord and flew across the model airplane flying field in Edwin Warner Park.

Gary Lanthrum went on to become a pilot with a Pitts Special, the "Porsche" of aerobatic toys. He taught me Beachey's moves one fine day above the Olympic Peninsula; I looped and twisted, flew inverted, danced, spun, and turned gloriously. All was exhilarating until Gary at last asked me if I would like to learn Beachey's stall recovery and

Gary Lanthrum and author at Cypress Lawn Cemetery.

his spinning dive of death, "the Beachey bore." I didn't last four seconds. It was the only time in my life that my stomach stopped me cold.

The story of Lincoln Beachey was daunting in an unexpected way. I had too much material to draw from: there were months, literally months, of uninterrupted reading. In writing this account, I had to leave out hundreds of anecdotes and incidents. In his time, Lincoln

Beachey was written about in volumes. Hundreds and hundreds of newspaper reports, dozens of magazine and newspaper feature articles, reams of communications and reminiscences were collected and processed. Much of this quaint "voice of the age" speaks for itself herein.

Both legend and historical record surround Lincoln Beachey—and hyperbole is infused throughout. Informed by Beachey's own confessions, interviews, and the accounts of the age, there are transitions where I blend a host of facts and reports and fictionalize a likely exchange and emotions, particularly in the first chapter as a child. But as much as possible, I let the contemporary report on Beachey's life and career testify to the sky-breaking phenomena of America's forgotten hero, the man who owned the sky.

GOSH!

Lincoln Beachey's last photo

LINCOLN BEACHEY
Daredevil of the Air
Souvenir Photo of Los Angeles Aviation Meet
January 20 – 28, 1912
Courtesy San Diego Aerospace Museum

Prologue

Lincoln Beachey's amazing life and staggering career is such an astounding piece of American history that it is even hard to believe at times. How could such an important trailblazer, who reached the absolute acme of American adoration fall so thoroughly into anonymity? What twist of fate turned this world-famous pioneer into "The Forgotten Father of Aerobatics"?

This story takes place at the turn of this century when the idealism of the age spawned a host of fellow heroes: Alexander Graham Bell, Thomas Edison, and Nikolai Tesla contributed monumental technological advances; Isadora Duncan recalled the dance of the ancients; Samuel Goldwyn and D.W. Griffith began to cast moving stories on the silver screen; Glenn Curtiss and the Wright Brothers began a new epoch in the air; Maria Montesorri breathed new life into children's education; Luther Burbank nurtured nature itself into new and vibrant forms; Henry Ford invented the assembly line and gave manufacturing innovative muscle. As these names flash across our collective memory, it is remarkable that one of their contemporaries, certainly the most popular luminary of his age, is now commonly unknown.

Because he died just before America entered the First World War, Beachey's memorials and historical accolades, local and national, were delayed—then eclipsed by heroes emerging from the war. He was lost amidst a new age. But while alive he was "known by sight to hundreds of thousands and by name to the whole world."

Lincoln Beachey performed for the largest audiences in the history of the United States. On his last tour of 126 cities in 1914, 17 *million* people saw him in one 30-week period. He made more than the national average *yearly* income every day he performed. The United States Congress adjourned twice from formal sessions, in 1906 and 1914, to witness his performances.

During his life he was compared to Milton and Michelangelo as well as to the leaders of his day. He was declared "the eighth wonder of the world" by a consortium of 100 newspapers. Even given the hyped-nature of the times, his fame was as vast as any in American history. His only fear was that he would be thought of as crazy and be forgotten. His only vices were "too many women" and an extreme boldness. His funeral in San Francisco was said to be the largest in the city's history. A national hero of colossal proportions has been unbelievably forgotten, and his iconoclastic story will re-write a bit of American history.

Consider the accolades of the 'poet laureate of the people,' Elbert Hubbard: "Each art has its master worker—its Saint-Gaudens, its Paderewski, its Michelangelo, its Milton. There is music and most inspiring grace and prettiest poesy in flight by man in the heavens, and posterity will write the name of Lincoln Beachey as the greatest artist on the aeroplane. In his flying is the same delicacy of touch, the same inspirational finesse of movement, the same developed genius of Paderewski and Milton. The deftness of stroke of any of the old masters cannot exact his touch. He is truly wonderful."[1]

Lincoln Beachey was hailed with superlatives: "The Man Who Owns the Sky", "Alexander of the Air", "The Genius of Aviation", "Master Birdman", and "The Divine Flyer". He was universally declared "The World's Greatest Aviator" by everyone from Orville Wright to Glenn Curtiss, from poet Elbert Hubbard to inventors Thomas Edison and Alexander Graham Bell. He received the regard of Presidents from Teddy Roosevelt to Calvin Coolidge as his acclaim reached the very peak of American hero-worship. Beachey inspired thousands to invest their lives in aviation, including Eddie Rickenbacker, Charles Lindbergh, General Curtiss LeMay, and five-star General Hap Arnold. He was personally and publicly credited with inspiring the reluctant U.S. government to build a force in the air.

Beachey's records and achievements speak of his time and his stature: he was the first man to fly upside down; first in America to loop the loop and the first in the world to master that stunt; the first man to tail-slide on purpose; he is the founder of stall-recovery, solving at last "the deadly spiral". Beachey was the first man to fly over Manhattan, Washington, Toronto, and scores of other American cities. He was the first to fly *inside* a building, the first to point his machine straight down and drop vertically until maximum velocity was reached, the first to pick a handkerchief from the ground with his wing tip. Such immaculate skill was necessary as he even invaded the canyons of downtown Chicago, dressed as a woman, dancing 'her' biplane wheels across car tops and cobblestones.

Lincoln Beachey's impact on aviation was enormous. He developed and perfected many of the fundamentals of flying. His aerobatic legacy is obvious. But his greatest impact was the demonstration to millions upon millions of Americans that flying machines were not only possible, but safe and practical. Beachey conveyed the ordinariness of flying by always piloting in common business attire, (only adjusting his hat to the reverse position) and then guided his flying into the roaring spectacular. He was America's Hero, for a while.

His glorious acclaim was perhaps best told in 1952 by the first biographer for the Air Force, Colonel Hans Christian Adamson:

> *It is hard to imagine* the adoration that followed Lincoln Beachey everywhere. He was DiMaggio, he was Lindbergh at his prime; he was all the stars of stage and screen combined, with a touch of Superman thrown in. From one end of the country to the other, he was known as The Man Who Owns The Sky.[2]

During the latter part of his career Lincoln Beachey earned enormous sums and planned to go into high-end design and aircraft development. But just after his twenty-eighth birthday, when he was being honored at the 1915 World's Fair for his decade of contributions to aviation, he drowned just inside the Golden Gate.

Notes

1. *San Diego Flying Days*, October-November 1913. The quote in this source is wrongly attributed to Glenn Curtiss.
2. Hans Christian Adamson, "The Man Who Owned the Sky" in *True Magazine*; February, 1953.

Accolades

I have watched him closely with my glasses and have never seen him make an error or falter. An aeroplane in the hands of Lincoln Beachey is poetry. His mastery is a thing of beauty to watch. He is the most wonderful flyer of all.

—**Orville Wright**, Dayton, Ohio, 1914

Each art has its master worker–its Saint-Gaudens, its Paderewski, its Michelangelo, its Milton. There is music and most inspiring grace and prettiest poesy in flight by man in the heavens, and posterity will write the name of Lincoln Beachey as the greatest artist on the aeroplane. In his flying is the same delicacy of touch, the same inspirational finesse of movement, the same developed genius of Paderewski and Milton. The deftness of stroke of any of the old masters cannot exact his touch. He is truly wonderful.

—**Elbert Hubbard**, world-renowned author, 1912

Lincoln Beachey is one of aviation's greatest pioneers. Quite a few of the early bird flyers were killed trying to emulate Beachey's aerobatic feats. Beachey was the first to determine that spins were the result of unintentional 'stalling' of the aircraft due to the loss of airspeed. He reasoned that one might recover from a spin by diving to regain speed, thus permitting control of the aeroplane. It took considerable courage to enter into an intentional spin, putting this theory to the test. Beachey's spin recovery technique did much to eliminate the fatal accidents that characterized those early days.

—**Dr. Paul E. Garber**, Historian Emeritus,
Smithsonian Institution, Washington, D.C.

LINCOLN BEACHEY
The Man Who Owned the Sky

Part way down the Fillmore Street Hill, looking northward from Broadway in 1908, thirteen years after Lincoln Beachey rode his bicycle down it. The two cable cars on this hill operated as counterweights; the descending car pulled up the ascending one.
Courtesy San Francisco Public Library

Lincoln's bicycle drop from Pacific Heights

Bird's Eye Map of San Francisco 1896

1

Fillmore Hill, 1896

Nine-year-old Lincoln Beachey looked past his rusty, over-sized handlebars, over the edge of Fillmore Hill, atop Pacific Heights. Another inch forward and there would be no turning back. Way at the bottom he saw Jimmy O'Guinn ride his store-bought bike to the back of the ascending cable car and grab on. He hated Jimmy O'Guinn; Jimmy did mean things to younger kids. O'Guinn was just the kind of snotty thirteen-year-old bully he would love to show up.

Lincoln looked to his right, into the eyes of his older brother Hillery. Lincoln could see both fear and admiration: even Hillery, who was almost twelve, wouldn't go off Fillmore hill with no brakes. But Hillery stood up to

THE BICYCLE OF 1896.

Jimmy O'Guinn and kept the bully from hurting his younger brother, taunted as the "little show off". Lincoln loved his older brother.

"Little", Lincoln thought. How many times he had heard that word; first grade, second . . . next month, fourth grade, and still the smallest person in the class. How he hated being called "little". Lincoln looked beyond the bottom of the hill, imagining himself flying through the flatland, all the way into Cow Hollow marsh with its fading filaments of morning fog. He gazed westward out beyond the marsh and bay to the Golden Gate—and beyond the gate where the sky and ocean blended seamlessly.

"Come on Linc, you can do it," the small crowd of admirers chimed. One of Jimmy O'Guinn's friends taunted, "Nah, Baggy Pants will crash, nyah, nyah, nyah." Jimmy O'Guinn, hanging onto the ascending cable car, had risen past Union Street and could see the hilltop quite clearly. Lincoln could tell, even from a hundred yards away, that Jimmy O'Guinn was giving him "the look".

Lincoln started to push off, but caution gave him pause. Only a few teenagers went off Fillmore hill without using their brakes. This was dangerous, and Lincoln Beachey was suddenly aware of his fragility and mortality. It would be silly to die just to impress foes and friends.

Lincoln took a deep breath, and remembered his skill—the months of practice going higher and higher, the bike tricks he did downtown on the vaudeville stage. He weighed his skill against the danger and knew he could do it, but it would take all his strength, all his concentration, all his confidence. This might be the last moment of his life ... but he didn't think so.

Lincoln swung his cap around brim-side rear, and focused on a distant point in the pavement far below. He did not seem to notice his admirers falling silent or Jimmy O'Guinn sitting upright to see. As he stood up on his pedals and began to roll off the edge, Lincoln fell into another reality of balance, focus, fear, and exultation.

Faster and faster, the drum of his tires shook upon the cobblestones and rose into shrill. Vallejo Street flew up at him like the blade of a scythe. Bamm! Pounding the horizontal bricks of the cross street shook his grip and another hill immediately fell below. He was already flying and barely holding on, and the next two drops would be even harder.

He could not help giving Jimmy O'Guinn a "look" as he zoomed toward him. But Lincoln was surprised to see admiration shining in Jimmy's eyes.

Suddenly, his bike pounded across Green Street and slammed his chin down onto his handlebars. Lincoln searched for his focus and clung to it with his very life. His feet went flying, his rear slammed upon the makeshift seat, but as he shot down the next drop, he somehow managed to hold himself balanced. At the end of Fillmore drop, Lincoln bolted across Union Street with such speed and control that he became airborne for a brief, timeless moment of exhilaration.

He had done it! The smell of smoke, Italian sausage, pasta and spices, horse sweat and dung at the bottom of the hill rushed into his nose and stung it with exhilaration. He was alive! Now he raised his hands in glory! Now he noticed the admiring girls and admiring men. The intoxication of applause swooned little Lincoln Beachey as he glided all the way down to the marsh beyond Lombard Street.

His mother had made his velvet nightgown from a curtain she got from a rich lady. It was like he was a prince. Amy Beachey got lots of material that way, since she did laundry for ten families, supplementing a paltry Army pension check each month. His nightgown was soft and oversized, comfortable and warm, like all the clothes she made for him. Getting under his army blankets, Lincoln studied his collection of wings; he delighted in his two best wings around his vaudeville award—giving it flight. He hoped he could perform on stage again. "Ten dollars, wow, " he thought, and figured how long he would have to deliver papers in Oakland to make ten bucks.

In the middle of the house, Lincoln heard his mother saying goodnight to Hillery. He could hear their words if he listened, but he wanted to think about the applause. He couldn't wait to tell his mom about his victory ride at the bottom of the hill.

"Well, Lincoln is nine, so he's been gone nine years," Lincoln suddenly heard the conversation. "He" meant Dad. Blind, in the Veteran's home in Dayton, wounded long ago as a boy soldier in the War between the States. Hillery was two and a half when Dad went to the Home. Hillery was writing Dad, maybe telling him about Fillmore hill. Hillery remembered their father, but to Lincoln he was just a picture and seasonal letters.

"Well, goodnight dear, sweet dreams." He heard Hillery's door shut and his mother's footsteps coming down the hall. He listened for her hand on the shiny black knob of his door.

The door opened and Lincoln saw his mother, round and warm, enter the converted back porch. She squeezed through the gap between the shelves and chest of drawers and sat on the edge of Lincoln's makeshift bed, fighting back her exhaustion one more time.

Lincoln did not notice her pain, so consumed was he with his own day. "Wasn't it great I did Fillmore hill, mom?" His eyes begged for praise. What could she say? She knew if she told him "No," it wouldn't stop him; maybe even, if he hesitated to think about her reluctance, it might hurt him. She remembered long ago teaching him to climb down from one thing after another. She knew he had probably practiced for months, as he said, but she would like to have known. If she said, "Yes", she would be encouraging scary feats. But there was no stopping him, so she awkwardly blessed him. "I'm always proud of you, and especially proud of how you prepare; it must be fun. You know it scares me a bit, but I trust you." Amy wondered only if she had said it right so he wouldn't get hurt.

Lincoln noticed that she wasn't as ecstatic as he was. He saw how tired she was, how she was still giving to him, through her tiredness and motherly fear. But he wanted to share the intoxication of his glory as he told her of his moment going off Fillmore hill.

Mom oo-ed, gasped, and ahhh-ed at all the right places and soothed his need for love. She folded the soft sheet across the rougher blankets and tucked the blankets closely around her little boy. He watched her hand cup around the sooty chimney, her mouth open, her lips pouting into a tunnel and, with a puff, the flame was out and she was gone.

He stared into the blackness, waiting for his eyes to get used to the dark. Lincoln knew his story was their story time. He thought of all the times Mom had read him *Darius Green and His Flying Machine*.

Dr. Otto Lilienthal, the first man to fly regularly.
Courtesy San Diego Aerospace Museum

Lincoln began to hum its sound and silly story. With his eyes relaxing into the dark, half the window frame appeared, then his collection of wings hanging from the ceiling like celestial visitors. Lincoln imagined flying, gliding and swooping like the birds, flying like Lilienthal the Berliner, or Chanute in Chicago. He delivered the newspapers. He had newspaper clippings of them. He pictured in his mind the flying machine Professor Langley and Alexander Graham Bell had flown. Next, they were going to fly one with a man in it. Lincoln could really imagine it; he had flown today.

Waking before the summer sun, Lincoln hurried to dress and fight the morning chill. Grabbing a piece of the coffeecake mom had made, he gently knocked on Hillery's door, "I'm going, see you later." He slipped out the door, grabbed his newspaper satchels, and was on his bike before Mom could say goodbye.

The fog was thin and the deep-blue sky still sparkled with morning stars. The chilly quiet was broken only by the jingling and clopping of distant delivery carts. The cold wind shook his bones and numbed his fingers, and Lincoln hurried to build up heat.

The *Examiner* building wasn't far, but Lincoln was warm by the time he got there. He grabbed his stack of papers and tokens, and headed for the Ferry building. The fog was thicker near the water, and soon he felt the morning's chill again. He watched the sky lose its last star to the brightening fog and perked his ears for the ferry. The rumble of the motor and splashing of the paddle-wheel sounded long before the vessel appeared mysteriously out of the fog. He paid one token to the ferryman and leaned his bicycle against the cabin. Walking between the carriages, wagons, and horses to the cables fencing in the boat's perimeter, Lincoln picked his spot, protected from the wind, near the front of the ship. The ferry cast off, made its turn and headed across the Bay. Lincoln settled in for his morning treat, enveloped in a cocoon of bright grey.

Gulls surrounded the ship, looking for the tiniest offerings, soaring above and dipping near the waves. He unwrapped his cake, broke off a tiny corner and threw it hard. Instantly, a gull darted and caught it easily just above a cresting wave. He marvelled at their exactness, their relaxed perfection, their immaculate timing. He became lost watching their every move.

The thirty minutes passed in an instant, only needing eleven crumbs. Best show in town, Lincoln thought, and for only eleven crumbs. Soon the ferry was docking at Key Route promontory, and the sun peeked over the Berkeley hills, reminding Lincoln how cold he was again. He opened the morning paper, August 10, 1896, to see the news he was spreading and felt even colder: across the Atlantic in Berlin, the first man to fly, Otto Lilienthal, was dead. On his tombstone his last words: "Sacrifices must be made."

Lilienthal's crash and death made it obvious to
Beachey what was at stake in taking to the skies.

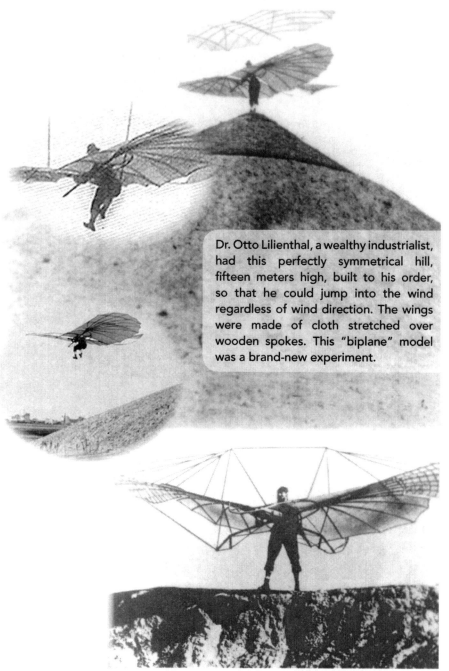

Dr. Otto Lilienthal, a wealthy industrialist, had this perfectly symmetrical hill, fifteen meters high, built to his order, so that he could jump into the wind regardless of wind direction. The wings were made of cloth stretched over wooden spokes. This "biplane" model was a brand-new experiment.

Lilienthal traveled to southern Germany to find cliffs suitable for his experiments with flight.

A Joke and a Waste of Time

For centuries, the saying "as difficult as flying" was used to denote impossibilities, and the very idea carried some form of ultimate *hubris*—boldly going into God's domain. Heavens! People feared that balloonists would incite the wrath of the Almighty, and even a century after the first French balloonists had dared to rise heavenward, belief remained strong that the sky was not man's domain. Still, men of craft and intelligence labored to build a winged flying machine, and late in the 19th century, technology began to catch up with the urge. So when Otto Lilienthal made regular, controlled, even beautiful flights in his bat-like hang-glider from 1891-1896, he made world news as the first man to fly. And if coasting through the air were possible, certainly someday the sky would be mastered.

America's champion of flying was the passionate and renowned Alexander Graham Bell. He studied Lilienthal's lift charts and notes, and passed that information on to Octave Chanute of Chicago, Samuel Langley of the Smithsonian, and every inventor and bicycle mechanic who asked for it. In turn, they passed their discoveries and theories back to him. Since his invention of the telephone in 1874, Alexander Graham Bell had poured a fortune into developing a workable flying machine.

Dr. Lilienthal controlled the lateral motion of his machine by shifting his weight from left to right and fore to aft. This method worked on a small scale.

In 1896, Bell and Langley seemed to be on the right track. They built a model 'quarter-size' *steam-powered* machine that successfully flew over 3000 feet, receiving high acclaim and sparking much speculation. Immediately they began working on a full-size, man-carrying machine and even Congress appropriated monies for the project. Langley was credited as the first person to produce a plane that flew on its own power.

In the mid-90's the bicycle became the national craze. The modern bike, with its brakes and geared pedaling, has its birth in the "safety bicycle" of 1891. In the cities, the means of personal transportation changed from animal to mechanical, from horse to bicycle, almost overnight. The safety bicycle triggered a dramatic change, even an epochal one.

1896 was also the year Lilienthal died. Outside Berlin, he was testing the glider he was planning to motorize when a sudden gust threw him down fifteen meters and broke his back. He went into a fever and died the next day.

If not for this freak accident, two bicycle mechanics in Dayton, Ohio, just might have grown up to be preachers like their bishop father. *News of Lilienthal's death set the Wright brothers thinking.* Twenty-nine year-old Wilbur Wright was convinced that the technological time had come for a manned, winged flying machine. He wrote Chanute about his beliefs and asked him for all his information on aviation. Chanute sent the Wrights the lift tables of Lilienthal's as well as research of his own. The brothers began to tinker and understand, experiment and invent. As with great duos, the dynamism of genius exceeded the sum of the partners. Orville and Wilbur had neither fortune nor formal knowledge to call upon, but a heaping dose of Yankee ingenuity and Protestant work ethic.

Otto Lilienthal had figured out how to hang on a wing and sail it through the air, but could not control it sufficiently. This problem would not be solved by professional engineers and theorists but by men familiar with balance and energy. The Wright brothers' days as bicycling enthusiasts gave them insight into solving this final problem of controlled flight. Using their cleverness *and* their bodies gave them a technical approach, albeit naïve: wing-warping like the birds, to sufficiently solve the problem of lateral control.

The 19th century ended with a new development that promised to change everything, perhaps even the heavens: the internal combustion engine. In 1899 the first horseless carriage went down Van Ness Avenue in San Francisco, and electric lights were put in its Western Addition. The world seemed poised to go into a marvelous new century. Twelve-year-old Lincoln Beachey knew what he wanted: to work on motors. He hung around shops and did chores for the men who took apart and re-assembled the magic machines, getting his education by apprenticeship. He quickly understood the new invention and soon became useful.

Lincoln could read and write well and do mathematics with excellence, but was bored in school. He knew enough about motors already. One day, at age twelve, Lincoln threw his books on a trash heap and told his mom he wanted to quit school and be a "mechanician," the most advanced job around. Amy Beachey took their $78 savings and bought Lincoln a broken-down engine. He fixed it, sold it for a huge profit and was on his way.[1]

By the autumn of 1903 the Smithsonian team had completed their flying machine. They had also built a new, greatly improved gasoline-powered motor and were ready to soar skyward. Langley planned to launch the four-winged airship—which looked like a dragonfly—from the top deck of a specially-built houseboat via a catapult over the Potomac river. The day arrived, the press came in droves, and Langley and Bell watched as the pilot, Charles Manley, who carried a compass in case he got lost, climb onto the machine. But the fragile craft collapsed upon launching and fell into the water like a giant wounded insect. Langley said the problem was in the catapult, and insisted they would try again as soon as repairs were made. The press scoffed, but not too loudly, for no one wanted to say that Professor Langley and Alexander Graham Bell were stupid! Still, at about that time, a highly respected American scientist named Simon Newcomb published a proof that powered manned flight was scientifically impossible.

In 1903 motorized vehicles were appearing more frequently on the streets of San Francisco. At fifteen, Lincoln Beachey had grown into a fine 'mechanician', and was among the first to take an old motor and attach it to his bicycle. He was a founding member of the S.F. Motorcycle Club. When he got hold of a high-performance Curtiss motor, legend has it that he terrorized the City with his speed.

1903 also marked a new horizon for Lincoln Beachey: he took his first ride in a tethered hydrogen balloon. In those days, Lincoln had an extra job, running a postering route, spreading the news of coming events. The day after his ride aloft, he threw his posters back—quitting suddenly —and announced, "You'll be putting up posters of me someday."

Back in Washington, on December 5, 1903, Langley's second attempt attracted legislators, public and reporters, but again the catapult damaged the fragile craft, "which fell like wet cement". Again the pilot had to be fished from the cold waters of the Potomac. This time the press howled, berating not just the inventors, but most of all, the very idea of flying. Washington newspapers trashed Langley, and concluded, "Yes, the problem of aviation will someday be solved, but after the combined work of millions and it will probably take thousands of years." Aviation was widely declared a joke and waste of money. On December 17th, *twelve days later*, no one, certainly no one in government, gave a second thought to the telegram from the bicyclist brothers at Kitty Hawk.

Langley's plane crashes into the Potomac, 1903

B ack in Dayton, the Wrights invited the press to show the world their great accomplishment, but bad weather hampered their efforts. Again the press berated the notion of flying machines and wrote off the Wrights. Left alone, they continued to develop the aeroplane, making longer and longer flights from a cow pasture just outside of Dayton. They wrote their congressman and the War Department, but only got standard 'thank you' letters in return. Now, instead of persisting in demonstrating their miraculous invention, the Wrights worked in secret, since their patent had not yet been issued. They became paralyzed with fear lest someone would steal their invention— and they be left penniless and not be given proper acknowledgment.

1904 should have been a banner year for aviation, but it stalled. The Wright brothers, worked into hysteria by their patent lawyers, stayed in hiding. When they were petitioned to bring their triumph out into the open, they announced righteously that God had chosen them as the inventors of the aeroplane, and until they were assured that every future flight made them money, their secrets would remain secret.

The Wrights inherited the work of many, added their own innovations, and put them together with great ingenuity. Indeed, their brilliant work deserved a patent, but they were wrong to claim, in effect, the very invention of the motorized glider. That had been done in 1896 by Bell and Langley, whose craft hung in the Smithsonian until after World War II as *the* first aeroplane.

1904 had its aviatic brights spots, however. Santos-Dumont, the brazen Brazilian of Paris, had circled the Eiffel Tower in a new kind of balloon, one that could be controlled like a ship in an ocean, that was *direct-able*, the *dirigible*. Santos-Dumont electrified Paris and vast crowds cheered his flights. His feat made headlines world-wide and won him the unheard of prize of $50,000. It also caught the eye of a premier San Francisco showman, Captain Thomas Scott Baldwin.

Born in the Midwest in 1856, orphaned at ten, Tommy Baldwin joined the circus in 1867, just after the Civil War. He leaped onto the San Francisco stage in 1877 when he parachuted (a radical new development) from a free-floating hydrogen balloon into the dunes of Golden Gate Park. In January 1887, at the age of thirty, two months before the birth of Lincoln Beachey, Baldwin again captured the imagination of San Franciscans and achieved national headlines by walking a cable strung from the Cliff House to Seal Rock. In 1905 he traveled to Europe to learn from Zeppelin and Santos-Dumont how to build one of those dirigibles. Self-appointed "Captain" Thomas Scott Baldwin had dollar signs in

Captain Thomas
Scott Baldwin

his eyes. In August 1904, back in California, the Captain made the first circuitous flight in the United States. He took off in his own dirigible from Oakland's Idora Amusement Park near 57th and Telegraph, flew out to the Bay and came back!

Baldwin rushed his machine to the World's Fair in St. Louis, where he had already secured a contract to exhibit the new flying wonder. If his machine could repeat a circuitous flight, he would capture the Gordon Bennett prize of $5,000. But in the thinner air of St. Louis, the dirigible would not lift him. He needed a lighter pilot, and quickly.

Baldwin met a young man who was flying captive hydrogen balloons at the Fair, and immediately offered his hand in friendship. He soon found out that young Roy Knabenshue was from a wealthy family who disapproved of his flying and circus life. But the boy knew how to sail the family yacht, and how to operate rope pulleys and a rudder. Baldwin was in luck. He offered Knabenshue a paltry sum to be his pilot, and Knabenshue enthusiastically accepted. After a two-minute lesson on navigating a dirigible, Baldwin sent him off on his first flight. Almost immediately the motor died, and Knabenshue was helpless.

Roy Knabenshue

The dirigible coasted straight toward one of the Exposition halls, miraculously glided past it, and then headed directly for the whirling Ferris wheel, which it also missed by inches. Poor Roy Knabenshue and the machine were recovered two hours later, twenty miles away in Illinois.

This near disaster discouraged neither Baldwin nor the young pilot. The next day, Knabenshue took the dirigible up again, circled the Exposition grounds, flew at 2,000 feet, covered three and a half miles in 28 minutes, and returned to the starting point "in an imposing manner," as one newspaper put it. He was greeted by a tidal wave of spectators, tossing their hats in the air, and was carried around the Exposition concourse on the shoulders of the mob. He had completed the requirements for the Gordon Bennett prize. After that Knabenshue dazzled the fairgoers daily, while Captain Baldwin took in piles of cash, most of which he kept. At the Fair's end, Knabenshue took his new knowledge with him and set up shop in Toledo, Ohio.

Notes

1. Hans Christian Adamson, "The Man Who Owned the Sky" in *True Magazine*, February, 1953

In 1908, Lincoln Beachey gets ready to board the undercarriage
of his dirigible held down by the assistants behind him.

Ancient Gods Were Speaking

Back in San Francisco Baldwin set up one Bud Mars to operate the cable of a captive hydrogen balloon down at the docks. Baldwin charged a whole $5 to see the world from heaven. Fortunately, seventeen-year-old Lincoln Beachey had won the City's motorcycle race and with his winnings immediately bought a ticket.

The Captain was clearly too old and too heavy to fly his own dirigible. He needed a pilot, someone small and fearless, who could scramble back and forth on the narrow trusses while hundreds of feet in the air. And that pilot needed to be an experienced mechanician as well, since his life might depend on knowing these high-performance Curtiss motors.

March 3rd, 1905 was Lincoln's eighteenth birthday. Being from the south of Market, he didn't expect much for his celebration. He was known for being proficient in mechanics, flawless in balance, and fearless on a motorcycle.

Captain Baldwin

17

His own reputation gave him a most exciting gift: an invitation to meet with Captain Thomas Scott Baldwin. Quickly, he talked it over with his older brother, Hillery, who had just returned from two years in the Navy. They came up with a plan for negotiating with Baldwin.

Lincoln had imagined that Captain Thomas Scott Baldwin's office would be bigger and nicer. It was almost as small as his childhood bedroom, a little box in a warehouse for Baldwin's dirigible. Papers were everywhere in piles, and Barnum-and-Bailey-like posters were half-stuck over all the walls. Plus, the

Hillery Beachey

Captain was fatter and older than his pictures showed.

"Well, I'll tell you, boys, because I won the grand prize in St. Louis, I can book as many venues as possible. But we've got to give the people a real show. I need a pilot and ground crew boss, and from what I hear, you boys would be perfect. I've got the contract for the Centennial Exposition of Lewis and Clark's expedition up in Portland, a real world's fair. It's the number one stage in America! I'll put up all the money to set it up, take all the risk myself, and I'll guarantee you each *three hundred dollars*, and ten percent of any profits after expenses." The Captain lowered his feet from his desk, took the cigar out of his mouth, bugged his eyes, and exclaimed, "Why, the sky is the future, and if your talents are half as good as your reputation, Lincoln, you'll be famous!"

Of all of his performances, paid and spontaneous, Lincoln suddenly remembered the intoxicating applause at the bottom of Fillmore hill. He forgot the aging Captain and the handsome money, and his little room and dark warehouse. He forgot Hillery standing beside him; forgot that something about the Captain's deal needed questioning. Lincoln heard each word resonate with the force of destiny, as if ancient gods were speaking through distant time.

Lincoln and his brother had a plan to enact if a deal was offered, and silence wasn't it. Hillery was eager for Lincoln to respond to the Captain, but Lincoln's reverie looked like negotiating strength to the Captain. "OK, ten percent for *each* of you, and I'll *guarantee* you three hundred and *fifty* dollars, that's a year's wage to some people, you know! But I can't risk any more than that, you can understand that, can't you?"

Lincoln suddenly was aware of the room, the situation, and the Captain's performance. Now he enacted the script he had worked out with his brother. "Well, I was figuring on a little bit more than that, how 'bout you Hillery?"

"I was figuring on a lot more." Hillery nervously asserted.

The Captain knew he had 'em. It was only a question of a trifle of money, compared to what he was going to make. "Look lads, I can't guarantee you any more than seven hundred dollars total, but I'll give you *twenty-five* percent of the profits after that, to split between you."

Lincoln appreciated the Captain's performance. To insist on a fairer deal would rock the boat, seven hundred dollars was a lot of money for two young men from the south of Market. This would get them start- ed. "OK by me," Lincoln appeared reluctant, but inside he was already flying, "if it's OK by Hillery."

In Hillery's eyes he could see the same fear and admiration he had seen since Fillmore hill. How hard it must be to look up to your lit- tle brother. But Lincoln also saw the joy of their partnership, and the delight that their plan had worked, even though both suspected the Captain had outplayed them.

"No, I think Lincoln deserves a one-hundred dollar bonus at the end of the show, since *he* is taking all the risks." Hillery suddenly strengthened; this was not part of the script. Hillery's time in the Navy had given him a new confidence. He surprised the Captain, who had thought the deal was in the bag.

Baldwin knew he had been outflanked, no matter how much he might protest. Hillery was quicker, and right. "Why, that's a marvelous idea, Hillery, and thoughtful, too. But let's make it fifty and we have a deal."

As they shook hands, the Beachey brothers were exultant, but held to Hillery's plan of seriousness and silence. The Captain inked the changes into the contract, and signed it with all the flair due the Declaration of Independence.

Baldwin quickly took charge again. "I've been performing and running shows for forty years, since I was ten. And let me tell you, the novelty and excitement of these flying ships and my talent for showmanship, together with your skills with ropes and netting, Hillery; and your fearless skills, Lincoln, why, we'll make a fortune. The people in the Northwest have never seen anything in the sky other than free-floating balloons. The dirigible is going to revolutionize the world! . . . Just sign right here boys . . . Someday, everyone will travel in one!!" The Captain had worked himself into a grand enthusiasm. "You will be the first to fly in the Northwest! And that's one big secret boys," the Captain said with conviction, "to be the first and best at what you do. We'll always find ways to set records. Your dirigible flying and record setting, Lincoln, that'll bring in the crowds, and we'll charge a whole dollar to take people up in the tethered balloon."

Just eleven days later on Tuesday, March 14th, Baldwin returned to Idora Park with his protégée and dirigible, and Beachey made his first flight. As he was landing, Baldwin was already selling tickets for an autograph to the rushing onlookers. In addition to flying knowledge, Lincoln began to understand how valuable the Captain really was. "Captain" Thomas Scott Baldwin was one great showman.

In Portland, Baldwin and the brothers set up shop at the Lewis and Clark Exposition of 1905. The Captain had the boys make a trial run of the captive balloon. Soon they were high above the Fair and rising through ceiling of morning fog. "Look, Lincoln, Mt. Hood!" Hillery exclaimed as they rose above the valley mist, but Lincoln had already seen it, and was focusing on another image to the left, in the farthest distance, an ephemeral triangle floating on the horizon.

"Yeah, and look north, see that purplish cone? You can just make out the snow line, that's Rainier I bet." Lincoln pointed as if he were shooting an arrow.

"Yeah, I see it, it's like it's floating to the left of St. Helens. Maybe you can see the snow line, and maybe you're just seeing clouds," Hillery responded.

Lincoln could see Rainier clearly. He remembered way back when he showed his mother that he could hit three marbles in a row with pebbles from his slingshot; his eyesight was beyond sufficient.

Suddenly, a distant voice below was bellowing to them, "OK, boys, that's it!" and almost immediately they felt the downward pull of the cable. Lincoln rode the shift of gravity as if he were performing a bicycle trick; Hillery held more tightly on the frame. They looked down at the Exposition, with its grand design, sparkling

PORTLAND AND THE LEWIS AND CLARK EXPOSITION

and pulsing. Now they saw Forest Park and the ridge glowing with the beginnings of fall colors, rolling west down the Columbia to the sea. Gazing southeast towards downtown, the ridge curves around and goes south up into the Williamette river valley. They could see their Fairmount hotel on the other side of the Exposition grounds, and in between the workmen finishing the preparations, exhibitors scurrying, and city officials promenading everywhere.

As soon as they were reeled all the way back down, the Captain whirled around and announced to the small crowd of insiders, "For all fellow exhibitors, officials, and other honored guests, coupons worth fifty percent off the advertised price of one dollar fee today only. One mile up, completely safe, who wants to be first? Come on, it's not too scary…" The Captain went on until a volunteer agreed to go up. Thereupon, a line quickly formed.

Lincoln and Hillery operated the jig to unreel the balloon quickly.

Beachey takes off at the Lewis and Clark Exposition
in Portland, Oregon, in September, 1905.

After the Captain counted his money, he gave Lincoln and Hillery each a whole dollar as a 'bonus'. He confided. "I'm doing this little routine for you boys, I want you to see how it's done. You see, practically nobody has ever been up in the air, and we give 'em the ride to heaven! It's a mile high to them, even if the cable is only three thousand feet," the Captain smiled like a child given a sucker. "Later I'll show you how we are going to positively rake them in off the avenue here."

The Captain worked the crowd and passed out coupons to every extended hand, and that was most of them. He turned to the Beachey brothers, directed and rehearsed their promotional scheme. "Lincoln, you stand here by the jig and basket and I'll be out here where our booth meets the breezeway. I'll say, 'See all of Portland from the sky! One mile up! One mile down! See the Williamette meet the Columbia! See distant mountains, look upon the glorious fair from on high!'... Or something like that... and I'll point 'em at you, Lincoln, and if it's a

Beachey rises slowly, using his weight to aim
the nose of the balloon upward.

couple, you look right at the lady and say, 'It's safe, thrilling, and educational', and smile politely, and if she smiles back you look right at the
guy and say, 'Don't worry, she'll be safe'.

"If they have any hesitation, Hillery, then you take this broom,
you'll be standing right here, and suddenly you'll start sweeping and
say, 'Move along please,' and sweep them right into our booth."[1]

The Captain's orchestration was superb. The Beachey brothers marvelled at his showmanship, his likable bravado, his cunning. He shaded
his manipulations by speaking seriously, as if in confidence, "Lincoln,
tomorrow is the opening. We need to fly the dirigible early, to draw
the crowds to our booth. Until yesterday, no one in the entire Northwest had ever seen a dirigible, only tethered balloons. Now you've set
a record, and captured a title. 'First Flying Machine and Aerial Pilot'
not just in Portland, but in the *Northwest*," the Captain emphasized.
"Every record is a title; and titles can make you lots of money. With

Lincoln Beachey approaches the Chamber of Commerce building in Portland, with a crowd waiting on the roof. The streets below were jammed with awed spectators. *Courtesy Oregon Historical Society*

our new Curtiss and new dirigible I'll bet you can set a speed record. Lincoln, I'm arranging the perfect day where you take the motor at top speed from here to the Oregonian tower and back. Like Santos Dumont in Paris! We'll track you and get something out of it, the press will love it. With your skills Lincoln, we'll top it off by delivering messages by air and landing on top of buildings downtown! Do you think you can do it?"

The Captain's inquiry was transparent. Of course he knew he could do it, and he wanted to—far more than the Captain did.

The Captain's performances inspired the Beachey brothers, and they set about their tasks with great energy… and the Captain was right. To the delight of Baldwin, Lincoln was a stark contrast to cautious Knabenshue: Lincoln was completely comfortable high in the air; whether 5 or 500 feet, Beachey would scamper like a squirrel and quickly acquired every conceivable skill. He "could make a dirigible do practically everything but turn somersaults."

Indeed, upon landing, when a newspaper reporter asked him if he was scared doing his aerial antics, Beachey replied with a wide smile, "I

When his balloon landed, Beachey became the first man in the world to deliver an air mail message via dirigible. He made the six-mile round trip from the Fair in a breathtaking fifty minutes. *Courtesy Oregon Historical Society*

was not nervous. I really liked the sensation. Some people instinctively like certain things, and I guess that is the way it is with me and the airship. I don't know what fear is when I am in the air."

The World's Fair of the Northwest was a stunning success, more than Baldwin had hoped for, and they took in a great stack of money. The Captain even got the Gelatin Company to pay for making the balloon, the world's first aerial advertising. Lincoln's flying was daring and superb. Thousands lined the avenues to watch. He set records (15 miles an hour!), and got high-profile press coverage by landing, message in hand, on top of *The Oregonian* newspaper building and City Hall, initiating airmail. And throughout it all, Lincoln luxuriated in the intoxicating acclaim. Young brothers, now heroes, were initiated into a covey of beautiful women.

The Captain received many lucrative offers for his dirigible, and decided to go into dirigible manufacturing. He would set up shop far south of Market Street in San Francisco, at the start of 1906, and let the boys work the circuit. It sounded like the perfect plan.

But when all the money was divided and the "expenses" tallied so that the Captain came out with the rest of the earnings, the brothers were not happy. They decided to join forces with Roy Knabenshue in Toledo. Lincoln and Hillery were smart not to tie their fortunes to the Captain. Just weeks later, Baldwin lost everything—his factory, his office, and ten dirigibles in production—in April 1906, when the earthquake and fire devastated San Francisco.

Knabenshue welcomed the Beachey brothers, and offered them a far better deal than Baldwin had. Lincoln helped Knabenshue build a dirigible, and was promised a lucrative spot as a pilot in the upcoming show in Columbus. But once in Columbus, Knabenshue did not relinquish his role as a star, and Lincoln was the back-up, and had to work as a member of the lower-paying ground crew. Bitterly disappointed, Lincoln and Hillery decided they knew enough now. They set out on their own.

Notes

1. *Reminiscences of Hillery Beachey,* Columbia University Archives.

LEWIS AND CLARK EXPOSITION
PORTLAND, OREGON
JUNE 1 – OCTOBER 15, 1905

Buying tickets at Capt. Baldwin's booth to see Beachey fly the airship (in distance).

BEACHEY'S AIRSHIP TOURED AMERICA

Beachey at New Bedford, Massachusetts, 1907

Beachey in the fields of York, Pennsylvania, 1907

Beachey over Baltimore City Hall, 1908

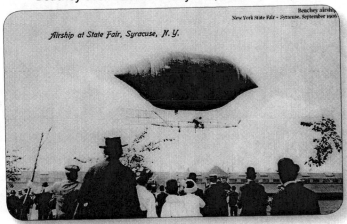

Beachey guiding his Airship over Syracuse, New York, 1906

The flimsy wooden undercarriage of the dirigible provided minimal footing for Beachey, who had to scramble back and forth to control ascent and descent. At altitudes up to 3,000 feet, this was no small feat. The balloon itself was made of oiled Japanese silk, covered with a netting to maintain its shape. Inside was highly explosive hydrogen gas, created by pouring sulfuric acid over lead. The entire apparatus, including the light spruce undercarriage and the motor, weighed only 210 pounds, plus a 140-pound pilot and 50 pounds of sand as ballast. The two-cylinder, four-cycle, five horsepower motor turned at 400 rpm.

Courtesy Hud Weeks Collection

Beachey buzzes the White House, September 10, 1906 — "Did you see it?"

Courtesy National Archives

"Did You See It?"

I t was bold. Maybe even stupid. It had better work. "OK, Hillery, we'll either be in jail tonight or toasting our success, but tomorrow the Beachey name will be headlines!" Without permission or fanfare, young Lincoln Beachey took off in the dirigible from Washington D.C.'s Luna Park on September 10, 1906. He would be the Capitol's first aeronaut.

As he cleared the treetops and headed toward the Capitol Mall, he began to hear excited screams below him. Within minutes, the news of a flying ship was on the wires. Buildings sprouted humans from the windows, roofs began to fill with people and a roar began to radiate from below him. Crowds gathered in thousands, business ceased, avenues swarmed, and shoppers, merchants and deliverymen watched open-mouthed as the dirigible floated over the summer streets. The City came to a standstill.[1]

Tacking hard into the slight breeze, Lincoln reached the Mall and turned toward the Washington Monument with the wind at his rear. The Mall was already packed end to end with a vast, throbbing mass. Tens of thousands of white handkerchiefs and dark hats shook below like multiple waves across a pond.

Lincoln circled the monument again and again in perfect control, proving to the thousands below the practicality of air ships. He was bursting with pride. Even though he knew he had accomplished the fame he and his brother had hoped for, the next daunting challenge captured his attention, the White House.

Hillery was already there. Inside, Mrs. Edith Roosevelt was talking to Dr. Benjamin Ide Wheeler, president of the University of California. As Lincoln approached the White House front lawn, he scurried forward on the trusses that pointed his ship down toward the lawn. He saw the guards running aggressively out to confront the intrusion, until Hillery jumped over the fence and temporarily distracted them. Like a sudden savior, Mrs. Roosevelt appeared and calmed the guards— and directed them to join Hillery and receive the airship's ropes. Nineteen-year-old Lincoln Beachey cut the engine and climbed down from the trusses, excited, even fearful about meeting the President's wife. A dream was about to become very real.

Edith Roosevelt and Dr. Wheeler walked toward the Beachey brothers. Hillery held on to the balloon, as Lincoln stepped forward. California's leading educator lunged forward and shook Lincoln's hand. "So good to meet you, young man," he practically shrieked.

The first lady stepped confidently forward, "Congratulations, young man, this is certainly the most novel call ever made upon the White House! Teddy is giving a speech at Georgetown and I'm sorry he couldn't be here. It's thrilling to see a man coursing through the sky. Have you shown this to Congress?"[2]

"No, ma'am, thank you, ma'am. I mean, no, Congress hasn't seen me, and I'm glad you like my piloting. Ma'am."

"Well, I think you should give our legislators a demonstration. You and your machine are quite marvelous. What is your name, where are you from, and who is your friend?"

Lincoln could not believe his luck: he missed the President, but the first lady was giving him permission to fly over the Capitol! "Lincoln Beachey, ma'am, and I-I'm from San Francisco. This is my brother, Hillery."

Beachey lets Congress see the thrill – and dangerous potential – of the new flying machines, September 10, 1906. *Courtesy National Archives*

The first lady could see that Beachey was uneasy and guessed he would be more comfortable in the sky. "Well, I'm so pleased to meet you and your brother, and may you impress the men on Capitol Hill."

Senator Bailey was addressing a joint session of Congress when a page ran down the aisles, yelling, "There's a flying airship outside, and it's coming right at us!!!" The staid politicians jumped to their feet and ran to the doors like little boys.

Filling the Capitol steps like a bleacher, the august crowd gaped skyward. Lincoln circled the dome several times and then dived toward the steps, separating the sea of men in suits. Lincoln Beachey landed his machine on the steps of the nation's Capitol and spent the next hour answering the questions from our nation's leaders.

"It is safe to say," reported the *Washington Evening Star,* "that there was not a full hour's work put in by any of the employees of the government or any of the other offices within view of the flight from 10 a.m. till after 12."

"Did you see it?" The query became so monotonous that people pinned little typewritten badges on their coat lapels that read, "I saw it."[3]

The Beachey brothers quickly got used to the adoring young women proffering their pleasures to the new heroes. In Ohio, Lincoln impulsively married the buxom May (Minnie) Wyatt. But Lincoln was not exactly ready for a wife. From his newfound sexual experiences, he had learned a different form of flying.

He soon abandoned the formalities of marriage and began allowing the adoring ladies to his hotel rooms as he continued to tour. Interestingly, it was considered not proper to engage in sexual relations unless one was engaged. Engagements can come and go, of course. Soon Lincoln was buying diamond engagement rings literally by the dozen—for which he became slightly infamous. He always kept one ready in his vest pocket for any amorous encounter. After a few months of touring, trying to hide both his wealth and his free sexuality from Minnie, he had a fiancée and a safety deposit box in most of the cities he visited.

Notes

1. *Washington Post,* June 17, 1906.
2. *Popular Mechanics,* August. 1906
3. *Washington Post,* June 17, 1906

With the Wright brothers keeping the lid on heavier-than-air flight, interest in dirigibles exploded. Knabenshue and Beachey were headliners at huge civic and entertainment events. 1907 was declared, "The Year of the Dirigible." Lincoln's dirigible flights after Washington were declared "the utopian pinnacle of modern sensationalism."

Before the Aeroplane, There Was the Dirigible

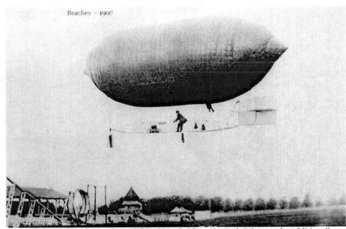

In October 1907 Lincoln Beachey exhibited his airship at the York Fairgrounds. Additionally, he flew over New York City, circling the Court House and the steeple of Christ Lutheran Church.

**As a budding American hero, Beachey had his portrait
made for publicity purposes.**
Courtesy San Diego Aerospace Museum

The Aeronautical Experiment Association

After the Wrights were granted their patent for lateral control, they continued their experiments in a hush until they had a contract with the government. They stifled development everywhere with their secrecy and also with lawsuits against all other flyers. They began to incite the wrath of the public. However justified the Wrights may or may not have been, their legal assaults "turned the hand of almost every man in aviation against them," as even their loyal associate, Grover Loening, later conceded. Editorials lambasted the brothers as selfish monopolizers. They were caricatured mercilessly in newspaper cartoons, one of which depicted them as pointing aloft and shouting: 'Keep out of my air!'[1]

By the end of 1906, a frustrated Alexander Graham Bell decided to form another group to build an aeroplane different from the Wright brothers', so that aviation could move forward. Bell gathered the top men in the field, and when he had to choose his number one man, the mechanician who would build the motor, build the machine, and probably pilot the craft, he went directly to motorman Glenn Curtiss.

Glenn Curtiss (1878-1930) grew up in the tiny town of Hammondsport, New York, on Lake Kekua, one of the "finger lakes". Like millions of other children, he worked on his bicycle to make it go as fast as possible. Across the upstate countryside, Curtiss trained hard, mastered his machine, and soon captured statewide awards for bike racing. Using his prize monies, Curtiss was able to acquire the new wonder: an internal combustion motor. He graduated to motorcycles, and soon began to design and craft his own light-weight high-performance powerhouses. In 1905, Glenn Curtiss set the world record for speed, 78 miles per hour, on his own motorcycle. The little town

The extraordinary Glenn Curtiss

of Hammondsport became world famous for its motors, sold to speedsters of all kinds—especially the weight-sensitive dirigibilists.

The next year, in 1906, Glenn mounted an eight-cylinder powerhouse onto a specially built bicycle frame and took it to Daytona. There was only one position to ride the machine: lying face down, arms almost straight back to the pointed handlebars. On this machine, designed for absolute straight-forward speed, Glenn was "the fastest man alive" as he exploded his own world record by bulleting across a mile of Daytona beach in 26.4 seconds—136.3 miles per hour, a world speed record that would stand for more than five years. "Only bullets are faster than Glenn Curtiss," the newspapers shouted. He later commented in his famous mono-

Curtiss on his record-setting motorized bike.

tone, "It satisfied my speed craving."[2]

Curtiss accepted Bell's offer to head up a team to build an aeroplane outside the claims of the Wright brothers. And so The Aeronautical Experimental Association was born. They hoped to make a public flight before the Wrights, and truly launch aviation in America. The Europeans had begun their leap into the sky and would soon overtake

Members of the Aeronautical Experiment Association gathered at Hammond-sport, New York, to discuss strategy. From left: Glenn Hammond Curtiss; Frederick (Casey) Baldwin; Alexander Graham Bell; Lieutenant Thomas E. Selfridge, U.S. Army; and John A.D. McCurdy. Selfridge became the first casualty of aviation; he was killed while flying with Orville Wright before the A.E.A. completed its work. McCurdy lived another fifty years, becoming a leader of Canadian aviation. Baldwin inherited the mantle of the childless Bell after Bell's death. Baldwin is often confused with "Captain" Thomas Baldwin, of dirigible fame, but the two were not related. *Courtesy of the Curtiss Museum*

America. *Scientific American* offered a thousand-dollar prize to anyone who would publicly demonstrate a flight of over one kilometer. While the Wrights had flown many times that distance, their desire for secrecy prevented them from coming forth to claim the prize.

Finally, on *the Fourth of July*, 1908, Glenn Curtiss flew the AEA's *June Bug* the prescribed distance and captured the coveted *Scientific American* prize. The designers established lateral control on their airship without warping the wings, as the Wright design had done, and, together with Santos Dumont, resurrected an idea the English Matthew Boulton patented in 1868: the aileron. This differently designed aeroplane could be made stronger and larger—since there was no problem with maintaining flexibility of the wings. Because of this first public demonstration of flight in America, Glenn Curtiss received the nation's first pilot's license.

The A.E.A. is successful: the June Bug flies one mile on July 4, 1908, capturing the Scientific American prize for the first public flight in America. Glenn Curtiss is the pilot. *Courtesy Glenn Curtiss Museum*

B y this time, the Wrights were being well received in Europe even at the very highest levels of society. The French, who had presumed that they were the world leaders in aviation lamented, "We're beaten," when they saw the Wrights fly. The brothers enjoyed a regard and success in Europe they had long worked for. Where the AEA had flown only a mile, the Wrights had stayed aloft for over *two hours*, covering 68 miles. They weren't worried about Bell and Curtiss or the Europeans.

But back in America, the Wrights seemed to meet only with misunderstanding, resentment, and disaster. They had one misfortune after another in dealing with the United States government. After the AEA captured the Scientific American prize, Octave Chanute convinced the Wrights to come out into the open and demonstrate their superior machines. They agreed to fly for the US government and meet the stiff requirements the government had established for air-worthiness, including carrying a passenger. Success would bring the Wrights $25,000 per aeroplane. The passenger was none other than Army Lt. Thomas E. Selfridge, a founding member of the AEA. On September 17, 1908, at Fort Meyer, Virginia, the Wrights expertly performed task after task for the dazzled officials, exceeding all the specifications the government required. But when Orville took Lt. Selfridge up, mechanical trouble caused the flying machine to fall 125 feet and crash, severely injuring Orville Wright and taking the life of Lt. Selfridge—the first man to die in an aeroplane.

Meanwhile, Lincoln Beachey continued to tour America again and again, as airships were the main attraction and most exciting feature of every public celebration. In November, 1908, following Philadelphia's popular Founder's Day celebration, *Aeronautics Magazine* told the story of the boy wonder and the absolute awe he engendered.

PHILADELPHIA. What seemed most remarkable to the great crowd that thronged the streets in answer to the call of the Founder's Week Celebration was the absolute control that the aeronaut Lincoln Beachey, who was in charge of the craft, seemed to exert, no matter how uncertain the wind appeared to those below.

A big military and naval parade had been arranged. The grandstands built all along Broad Street were jammed with men, women, and children. The pavements were banked solid to the curb. Far up Broad Street could be seen the advancing parade. The crowds waited with bated breath.

Then, suddenly, out of a lot on Wallace street, where throngs were thickest, there rose the airship, slowly, gracefully, and swanlike. Like a spider, the aeronaut could be seen balancing his ship as it rose into the air by moving backwards and forwards.

Then, pausing for a few moments over a high building, the airship waited until the first ranks of the big parade approached and proceeded just ahead of it, down Broad Street. The crowds actually forgot the parade in the excitement of watching the dirigible balloon. They arose en masse and waved hats and handkerchiefs. They cheered and shouted. Mayor Reyburn, sitting in one of the grand-stands, wildly waved his high hat. Governor Stuart, rid-ing a horse in front of the parade, pulled up on the reins and halted the entire pageant for a few minutes while he gazed up at the airship.

At various points along the procession the crowds broke through the ropes and poured into the street so that they might get a better view of the steed of the air. Mounted policeman had to drive back the crowds . . . [3]

Fly Magazine reported on the personal impact of the young aeronaut.

A boy of 21, slenderly built, quiet in dress and manner, and low of voice, inconspicuous in a crowd; almost, one would say—inconsequential—until one noted the clean, firm jaw, and suddenly looked into the dark-lashed, blue gray eyes of so extraordinarily steady and intrepid an expression that any student of the faces of men would identify them instantly as belonging only to some fearless explorer, some adventurer into the unknown, dangerous, uncharted space. Livingstons' eye burned with the same fire; so did Landor's who endured torture that he might enter the mysterious walled city of the Dalai Lama in the heart of the Himalayas. The voyagers who have come home again from the Frozen North carry the same look, —the expression of the men who count danger, suffering, self-sacrifice, life even, as nothing if they may but add a word or two to the unwritten pages of the world's great Book of Knowledge. To join this valiant company now comes the Pioneers of the Air; and this quiet boy Beachey, who by the earmarks of him, is one of the Brotherhood.

To mount into the heavens astride a skeleton frame-work, to dive and soar and wheel in circles, to beat into the wind and keep one's balance in the heavier gust, with

THE AIRSHIP. Its Builder and Operator. Founders' Week, Philadelphia, 1908.

Lincoln Beachey flew at the Founders' Week celebration in Philadelphia in 1908, wearing military headgear rather than his customary cap with a bill. He flew his dirigible out to one of the ships docked in the Delaware River, and delivered the world's first air-to-ship message to a sailor waiting in the crow's nest.

Courtesy San Diego Aerospace Museum

only the air and lateral rudder, calls for the spirit and imagination of an entirely new order. And so, one no longer wonders that Beachey, daring to explore unknown upper regions, is yet afraid of people, especially those laudatory, curious and enthusiastic folks who ask eager foolish questions and gape in awe.[4]

Even though heavier-than-air machines were now more than five years old, very few people had ever seen one. Reports of aeroplane success were regarded with extreme skepticism or disregarded completely. Fortunately, the fundamental logic of the lighter-than-air ship was clear to anyone; the wonder of the day was in the navigation and control of the airships. Lincoln Beachey and Roy Knabenshue were America's top heroes of the sky, and the dirigible seemed to be the only real hope for manned flight.

Notes

1. Curtis Predegast, *The First Aviators*, Time Life Books, 1980.
2. Roseberry, C.R. *Glenn Curtiss: Pioneer of Flight*.
3. *Aeronautics Magazine*, November 1908.
4. *Fly Magazine*, December 1908.

America's first aviation show at Dominguez, California – January 10-20, 1910
Beachey as master pilot on the fast-becoming "old-fashioned" dirigible.

A New Epoch

In 1909, Europeans were electrified when an aeroplane crossed the English channel. The French aviation club, led by the famous Tower builder, Gustav Eiffel, decided to hold a party like no other: the world's first aviation meet, to be held in ancient, elegant Rheims. Each country's representatives would compete for prizes and records, with the victor earning the eventual title of world champion. The Wright Brothers, who had demonstrated that their machines were the most developed, were invited to represent America. In deference to the Wrights' achievement and expecting them to be the champions, the trophy was already cast in the shape of the Wright Flyer. But at the last moment the Wrights withdrew, citing legal disagreements and moral principles. "God does not approve of competition and circus performances like this do no good for the science of aviation." They sent instead their lawyers, who brought suit to confiscate aeroplanes other than their own, and burn them as violations of their patent. They wanted a percentage of every aviatic event without even showing up.

The committee directed their lawyers to deal with the Wrights, and sent an immediate wire to Glenn Curtiss asking if he had a machine ready and was willing to come. He had almost finished building one (the fruit of all their early experiments), but had not flown it. To take it to an international competition was a huge opportunity—but with an untried machine? Without him, America would not be represented. He agreed to immediate travel.

Glenn had great faith in his craft, and although there were comparable European aircraft, his familiarity with high-performance machines gave him confidence. He was sure that he and his Rheims Flyer would do well. In that first-ever meeting of the world's aviators, Glenn Curtiss dazzled the other flyers with his high-angled turns and powerful motor, and emerged the champion. He ironically received the silver Wright biplane atop a figurine as his trophy. Returning to New York City, Curtiss basked in a gigantic hero's welcome with a grand naval flotilla leading his victorious entrance into the city.

In November 1909, The Wright Company was incorporated with a blue-chip directorate, including August Belmont, Cornelius Vanderbilt, Robert Collier, and others of comparable wealth and influence. The Wrights received $100,000 cash outright, forty percent of the stock and ten per cent royalty on all planes sold. Wilbur Wright was named president.[1]

Curtiss's friends soon convinced him to hold the first aviation meet in the United States, directly challenging the Wrights' claim of aerial ownership. He was the champion, and would defend his title. With winter approaching, arrangements were made for the First American aviation meet, to be held just north of Long Beach, California, on a mesa called Dominguez. Pilots, equipment, and inventions came from all over the world: balloons, dirigibles, and actual, practical aeroplanes. For the first time in America, you could pay a dollar and see every kind of flying machine!

The Wright brothers chose not to compete in Los Angeles, but they made their presence well known. When the French aviator Paulhan stepped off the liner from France, lawyers in New York served papers informing him that the Wrights had filed for an injunction to keep him from flying in the United States. Moreover, a week before the Los

Angeles meet, a federal judge granted the Wrights' request for an injunction against Glenn Curtiss as well. Curtiss posted a bond, appealed the ruling and, in the face of legal repercussions, decided to go ahead with the Dominguez meet.

Tens of thousands gathered that first day, January 10, 1910. In the crowd, betting pools began to form, with odds five-to-two against any heavier-than-air flying machine actually flying. William Randolph Hearst was there for the *Examiner* newspaper, with Samuel Goldwyn filming the event. A businessman named Boeing came from Seattle to see if the flying machine stories were actually true. Tens of thousands were eagerly anticipating that they might see the impossible, including fourteen year-old Jimmy Doolittle, the eventual father of strategic bombing.

The heroes of the day, 1910. Front row, from left; Hillery Beachey, Col F. K. Johnson, Glenn Curtiss, Louis Paulhan, Charles Willard, Didier Masson, Lincoln Beachey (third from right), Roy Knabenshue, and Charles Hamilton. The photograph suggests that these aviators knew they were making history.

Glenn Curtiss opened the show. The crowd began to hum, and the band began to play. The famous Curtiss motor was kicked on, and the machine began to roll and everyone in the crowd stood and began to shout. The plane rolled quickly across the field and suddenly leaped into the air. In was reported that the most notable quality about this moment was the absolute silence: the rising roar of the crowd and the throbbing pulse of the band all suddenly stopped. The silence was broken only by a single motor and wings rising into the sky. A sea of muted mouths gaped in disbelief, and some band members dropped their instruments. Each spectator was forced to re-arrange the old of ways of thinking. The idiom "As impossible as flying" ended that January day. As the re-alization that a new epoch had begun became stunningly obvious, the silence was shattered as waves of acclaim hit Curtiss, roaring and rum-bling like rolling thunder. Lincoln Beachey, who was at Dominguez with his dirigible, heard the bursting of his ballooning career.

But it was the Frenchman Paulhan who stole the show. He brought two Farman monoplanes, two Bleriot monoplanes, two me-chanics, a French wife, a French car, a scarf, and a poodle. He was determined to outshow Curtiss and everybody else. He would not fly simply and safely like Curtiss, but swoop and dance with grace and French style. Day after day, he daz-zled the crowds, and outrageously mocked Lincoln Beachey's victory over Roy Knabenshue in the dirigible race by flying circles around the slug-gish balloons. In the Farman, Paul-

The dashing Louis Paulhan, left, posed with America's No. 1 aviator, Glenn Curtiss, at the Los Angeles meet in January 1910.

han climbed to a new world-record altitude of 4,165 feet; he flew to Santa Anita racetrack and back (45 miles!), and won $19,000 of the prize money, over twelve times a good annual wage.

The *Los Angeles Daily Times* reported that mankind's most elusive dream had come true.

LOS ANGELES DAILY TIMES.

VOL. I.   LOS ANGELES, CALIFORNIA,   JANUARY 11, 1910   NO. I.

W E   F L Y !

It is no longer a question whether we can fly. The question now is to what end and to what purpose shall we steer our flight?

What shall we do with this new and wonderful gift?

The airship has arrived. It is not a problem nor an inventor's dream. It is here. Aqui!

From the Aviation Field one carries away an impression of the easy superiority of the aeroplane to the forces of gravity. For many centuries "as difficult as flying" has been the figure of speech to denote impossibilities. But, when one witnesses these marvelous machine-birds in the act of flying, the surprise is that it seems easy, not difficult.

Its war possibilities are the puzzle and dread of every civilized Army. Most experts seem to agree, however, that the weight-carrying possibilities of an aeroplane are mathematically limited to slight burdens [based on wing-warping]. Probably it can never be used commercially. But the dirigible may rival the ocean liner.

The aviation meet at Los Angeles is not merely one of the events of the year: it is an event of the age; it is epochal.[2]

People were overwhelmed by the sight of flying machines and understood that a new day in human history had dawned. After the Rheims event, Count de Lambert wrote, "The day on which man in his primitive form crawled out of the water and found he could move and live on land was no more of an epoch than this." Along with everyone else, Beachey marveled at the flying machines, read the newspaper coverage, and clearly saw the end of his dirigible career. "Gas bag doings

Enormous crowds looked up at what they could hardly believe; men flying winged machines, at America's first Aviation Meet in Los Angeles, 1910.
Courtesy San Diego Aerospace Museum

have become commonplace. The aeroplane is the real thriller."

On February 17th, a federal judge granted the Wrights' injunction and forced Paulhan to cancel his tour. In New York City, before departing back to Europe, he flew a few times free, thumbing his nose at the Wrights.[3]

Wilbur retorted, "We made the art of flying possible, and all the people in it have us to thank." Unfortunately, by mid-1910, the Wrights were putting much of their energy into legal fights, and aviation suffered both from their absence and from their attacks.

Notes

1. Curtis Predegast, *The First Aviators*, Time Life Books, 1980
2. *Los Angeles Daily Times*, January 11, 1910
3. Pendergast, Ibid.

New Era of Flight

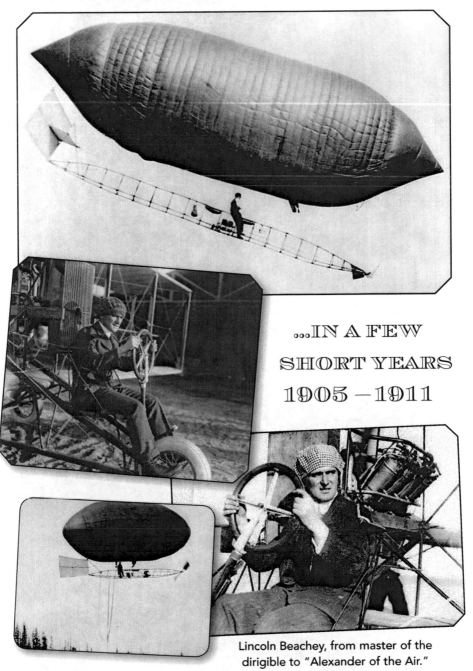

...IN A FEW
SHORT YEARS
1905 – 1911

Lincoln Beachey, from master of the
dirigible to "Alexander of the Air."

BEACHY READY FOR FLIGHT IN BIPLANE
BENTON HARBOR, JULY 17-18-'12

LINCOLN BEACHY STARTING HIS BI-PLANE

LINCOLN BEACHY

Lincoln Beachey,
one of the most
photographed persons
of his era.

Glenn Curtiss, who held American Pilot's License No. 1
Courtesy Glenn Curtiss Museum

The Silent Chill of Death

"**M**r. Curtiss, pleased to meet you, I'd like to join your flying team." Beachey was certain this was a formality. His four years of touring America made him think highly of himself and his name.

"Well, I don't need another pilot right now . . . that is unless you can fly . . . an aeroplane, that is." Lincoln was stunned into silence. Curtiss was strictly business, and his condition remained: first fly, then maybe Lincoln could join. He could fly only if he could already fly. Greatly disappointed, Lincoln and Hillery left Dominguez, determined to build themselves their own flying machine.

At thc Indianapolis Motor Speedway on June 17, 1910 was the Wright team's inaugural exhibition. The Beachey brothers brought a primitive monoplane of their own design. The best report of the 'flight' said that it rose eighteen inches before Lincoln crashed into a fence.

Hillery wanted to devote time to aircraft design and construction, but Lincoln was too impatient to reinvent the aeroplane. They decided to part ways. Very soon Lincoln swallowed his pride and went to the Wrights.

"Yes, we would be glad to take you, Mr. Beachey: that'll be $500 to

Lincoln Beachey is ready to fly an early Curtiss Pusher, with the propeller facing backward, as was typical of all American flying machines of the time. Just behind the pilot is a large radiator for the water-cooled engine. The triangular flap in front of Beachey's feel, an early attempt at a rudder, was soon discarded from the design. *Courtesy San Diego Aerospace Museum*

learn and then you get ten percent of the take." Lincoln could not believe his ears—Captain Baldwin suddenly seemed generous. The Wright brothers were as bad as he had heard. Didn't they know who he was?

Lincoln knew he couldn't go back to dirigibles, and he couldn't go forward into aeroplanes. He tracked down Glenn Curtiss on the Midwest circuit and petitioned him to take him on as a mechanician. Curtiss agreed and eventually gave him his first airplane ride on the Fourth of July weekend over Atlantic City. It was reported that Lincoln stood on Curtiss' seat behind him, holding on with only one hand while waving to the cheering crowds.

Back in Hammondsport, Lincoln convinced Curtiss to let him take up a machine by himself. Lincoln imagined soaring up and down Lake Kekua and the exhilaration he would soon know. So eager was he to take to the sky that he pointed his machine upward at too high an angle, stalled, and immediately crashed tail first into the ground.

Miraculously unhurt, he muttered some excuse about how surprised he was by the controls being so responsive. Everyone, including himself, knew he would fix the wreck in his own time and try again. The second time was no different. Neither was the third. Curtiss ordered him to be fired.

Curtiss' promotional wizard Fancuilli defended Lincoln. Knowing that the name of Lincoln Beachey would draw crowds, he convinced Curtiss to give Lincoln another try.

Beachey was a poor pilot at first and blew most of his landings. He couldn't get the full feel of the machine and spent most of his free time and salary repairing landing gear.

By December of 1910, Lincoln could claim moderate control of his flying machine, but he was still far more useful as a mechanician than pilot. Legend has it that his flying, and the flying of all future pilots, was suddenly transformed when Curtiss took Lincoln (as a mechanician) and fearless ace flyer, Charlie Hamilton to a flying exposition in Los Angeles.[1]

The buffeting wind played havoc with the aeroplanes that legendary day. A Wright plane went down and the crowd hysterically attacked the fallen bird, grabbing pieces for souvenirs — even tearing the clothing off the bloody body of the pilot. It took the police to break up the mob and remove the corpse. Lincoln couldn't help but notice the dark side to the crowd and wondered if that unglamorous corpse would be him someday. Every aviation event had gambling pools, with the odds against the flyers living out the day.

Charlie Hamilton was fearless because he had tuberculosis. He commented regularly (and correctly), "I'll die in bed." Before each flight, he took a swig or two of whiskey and took off. The freak wind also tossed him down, but he managed to hit on his landing gear. Critically injured, he was rushed to a hospital, but the plane had only minor damage. A mechanician spoke to Curtiss, "I can get this plane fixed in ten minutes. Fly it again, let those businessmen know your planes are tough. The Wright plane fell to pieces."

Curtiss thought about the expense of his trip—he would need to sell some planes—but it would look bad for him to step down into the piloting position. "But who's going to fly it? Beachey?" he said jokingly.

Lincoln whole-heartedly accepted his assignment to fly. He took off in blustery winds, fighting to impress his boss and to stay alive. The wind continued to buffet the aircraft, and Lincoln found that holding the controls tightly only made things worse. He tended to over-correct for each gust, and the over-tight control placed him in more jeopardy than the wind. When he forced himself to relax, and let the airplane's natural stability compensate for the bumpy ride, things began to look up. The deafening roar of the motor strained against the wind and gravity, as Lincoln rose to three thousand feet. He was so happy he began to sing aloud. But he was interrupted by a swift silence: the motor had stopped.

"The silent chill of death raced across my soul as the aeroplane began to fall out of the sky," Lincoln later recalled.[2] The crowd leapt to their feet in anticipation of another souvenir. Every pilot there knew there was no escape from the "deadly spiral"; they were all about to witness the death of Lincoln Beachey.

With his heart in his mouth, Lincoln prepared to meet his demise. It would all be over soon, one way or another.

Lincoln was taken by a new phenomenon: it was quiet! The motor wasn't overwhelming him and he could feel the entire aeroplane as it plummeted toward earth. He was powerless and falling towards the spinning ground.

Somehow, for some reason, instead of reacting in terror, Lincoln remembered back to the hours and days of watching the seagulls around the ferry and called upon their knowledge. He relaxed beyond his fear as he visualized the ferry gulls.

The natural reaction in a spin is to grab the controls more tightly and try to pull out of the spin and up from the dive, but that only seemed to make the spin faster. Out of Beachey's seagull contemplations, suddenly Lincoln realized he needed power or his controls were useless. Against every natural tendency, Lincoln nosed his aircraft *into* the fall, facing death instead of jerking away, and dove into it as simply as any gull. Like a bird, he quickly had enough power from this dive and the controls stiffened and began to respond; he was able to pull up at the last second. He coasted across the field and set his machine down with the majesty of a California condor, the world's first 'dead stick' landing. Not since Dominguez had Beachey heard the crowd roar as it did on this occasion.

Curtiss was the first to reach him as Lincoln climbed from his machine. "Linc, that was as fine a demonstration of flying as I've ever seen. You beat the deadly spiral! Thank God you're alive."

"Mr. Curtiss, in the silence I could finally feel the whole machine for the first time. I think I know how to fly now." Lincoln was sure he had found the door he was looking for.

Notes

1. Hans Christian Adamson, "The Man Who Owned the Sky" in *True Magazine*, February, 1953.
2. "The Pacemaker for Death" by Lincoln Beachey.

Lincoln Beachey circling Flag pole with both hands free from steering gear

Lincoln Beachey demonstrates his feel for his plane by combining flying with no hands and daring showmanship.

They Came to See Him Die

Three weeks later, everyone in aviation was up the coast in San Francisco for the Tanforan Aviation Meet. Lincoln Beachey entered his first competition as a 23-year-old novice in his hometown. There would be competitions in racing, record setting (altitude, distance, etc.), taking off and landing in the shortest space, accuracy, new ways to use an aeroplane, and showmanship. His newly acquired feel for the plane gave him an edge over the other aviators. He would see his mom, friends, and his wife, May. He hoped the necklace and earrings gift would help her believe him.

At the meet, one of Curtiss' top flyers, Eugene Ely, began naval aviation by landing and taking off from the deck of the *Philadelphia* floating on San Francisco Bay. Military leaders were equally impressed by the world's first bomb drop. But legend has it that by the third day of the meet, no other flyers would compete against young Beachey for fear that he would

Eugene Ely begins naval aviation on San Francisco Bay, 1911.

make them out to be amateurs. At this humble aviation meet, true flying was first seen, where only glimpses were before.

Miss Shea, of Bridgeport, Connecticut, having won a ride with Lincoln Beachey, sits calmly on a wing, with no seat belt or other restraint. Whether her knuckles are white can not be discerned in this picture. The bamboo framework slanting upward in front of Beachey held a forward horizontal "wing," thought to be necessary for altitude control. Beachey later broke it, and the discovered the plane flew better without it! *Courtesy San Diego Aerospace Museum*

One of the curious young women in the grandstand asked her escort how much Beachey was paid for winning the shortest take-off event—which only took two minutes of his time. "One thousand dollars," was the answer. "My," said she. "That's an easy way to earn all that money, a year's sum to many." Then after a few minutes of silence: "That's thirty thousand dollars an hour—more than Rockefeller! I wish I were an aviator."[1]

Curtiss booked Beachey on a East Coast tour, starting in the Caribbean with Puerto Rico and Cuba (first aeroplane in both places). While Lincoln had gained a real feel for his machine, he was still learning; that is, still making errors. On January 29, 1911, Lincoln narrowly avoided smashing the Curtiss Flyer into an automobile in which sat the

Lincoln Beachey took his flying machine by ship to Puerto Rico, where he re-assembled it and flew before a crowd of admirers.
Courtesy San Diego Aerospace Museum

President of Cuba and his family, but couldn't avoid crashing into another auto parked a few yards away. He would catch up with the rest of the team in August, at the huge meet in Chicago. On his tour, he continued in the style of Captain Baldwin, setting records in many places just by showing up. It was also newsworthy that even at a rough place like a racetrack, half of Beachey's following was female; this fact alone was positively scandalous, even if advantageous to Lincoln.

He worked daily to develop long steep drops, to feel the stresses and reaction times. The press and public loved it, saying: "Driving his aeroplane to a height of 600 or more feet, Beachey glided in a spiral fashion almost to the earth, and as the machine was about to touch the ground he pointed its nose upward, and a few minutes later was again near the clouds. This was done repeatedly." The growing crowds loved his antics.

In Tampa he attached acetylene lamps to his wings and initiated night flying. Then, early in May 1911, twenty-four year-old Beachey and McCurdy arrived at Washington D.C. for a meet at the Benning racetrack. He completed all the requirements for Pilot's License #27, which was witnessed by the Press, who reported the various requirements "seemed to be an easy matter for Beachey, and, as the last number on the program, he made his aeroplane do every antic known in the world of the air."

On a lark, Beachey left the racetrack and made a flight past the Capitol, the first to do so. Minnesota Congressman Lindbergh was there with his twelve-year-old son, Charles, who excitedly witnessed the fly-by.[2]

The people of New York stood in still awe of the first aeroplane to fly over the Manhattan skyline. During this flight, "Broadway lay as quiet as a country lane."[3] At a time when monthly wages averaged $100, Lincoln earned $5000 by winning the Gimbel's Department Stores race from New York to Philadelphia, a flight "witnessed by millions."

It was reported that when he landed before a crowd estimated at 100,000 and received his fortune, Beachey was "warmly greeted" by one Mae Wood, who was dazzling in a stylish purple hat and a purple-and-white gown. Minnie Beachey had obviously returned home already, for Miss Wood,

Beachey and Miss Mae Wood. Elmira-August.1911.

who gave her age as nineteen, rode with Beachey over the entire summer of 1911. Reporters tactfully excused her close companionship with the explanation that she was "taking lessons on the management of the air craft."

Lincoln also changed the shape of early aeroplanes in America. When

Beachey crashed into a fence on June 2 at Wilkes-Barre, Pennsylvania, he damaged his front elevator. He had seen the Wright's removal of the front wing just a few months before. Instead of taking time to fix the front wing, Beachey simply removed it. He found he could indeed fly in a much freer manner after adjusting to the "headless" configuration.[3] To prove his point, Beachey strapped a motion picture camera beside him and managed to fly and crank the camera at the same time. It is said to be the first movie footage ever shot from an aeroplane.

Curtiss heard about Beachey's removal of the front wing and steamed, "So far, we have been extremely fortunate in not having any accident happen to the men or spectators, but we cannot hope for this good luck to continue long when we consider how Beachey is flying."

Even now, a year and a half after Dominguez, aeroplanes were still mythical to most Americans, something they had only read about in some big city far away. Such reports seemed utterly fantastic. One actually had to see flying machines to believe them to be real. In addition, aeroplanes did not have a good reputation: in early 1910, one in three flights still ended in disaster. This suspense affected crowds everywhere.

The mighty Niagara Falls, the most powerful natural landmark in the United States on the border with Canada — the Horseshoe Falls on the Canadian side, the American and Bridal Veil Falls in the U.S. — had held a morbid fascination for Americans for centuries. Its power was immense, the water a torrent of danger. Since the late 1800s, men and women (the first to survive being a woman) were bravely plunging over the Falls in barrels, or metal "caskets," to gain fame and glory. Now in 1911, the master magician Harry Houdini was scheduled to tight rope walk over the roaring cataract, if he could get legal permission. Lincoln Beachey arrived on his exhibition tour to try what no one else had even dreamed: flying over the Falls down the gorge to rise out of the mists to worldwide fame... and a good deal of money! Beachey's raced ahead of a storm as he arrived in Niagara Falls, which was well reported in the *Cataract Journal*:

THOUSANDS WITNESS HIS ARRIVAL AND ATTAIN FIRST SIGHT OF AN AEROPLANE

June 26, 1911. Thousands of Niagara Falls people, and tourists who spent Sunday here, obtained their first view of an aeroplane yesterday afternoon when Lincoln Beachey, the daring young aviator engaged for the International Carnival, arrived in the city from Buffalo via the air route! Long before 4 o'clock every available place near the Robinson tract at Twenty-ninth street filled with an eager throng anxiously awaiting their first glimpse of the most wonderful of all inventions. Hundreds of automobiles filled the adjoining streets and the rich and poor alike mingled in a good-natured struggle for vantage ground.

It was 4:32 o'clock when the cry, "Here he comes," echoed from thousands of youthful throats and from older ones as well. Throughout the wait the humorists in the crowd had been busy with false alarms, but this time Beachey really made his appearance in the southeast, against a heavy black cloud, flying about 1,200 feet high. In a few brief seconds—too soon altogether to satisfy the crowd— he landed as gracefully as a bird in the spot he had selected. The ground is rough, but so skillful is the aviator that he picked out the most adaptable site and his machine was scarcely jarred.

Amid cheers from thousands of throats Beachey was out of sight. The members of the Carnival committee at once surrounded him to offer congratulations. To them he said:

"It was a fine flight, but the rockiest cross-country trip I have ever made. The wind was playing all sorts of pranks. Far up—about 3,000 feet it was puffy and gave me a lot of trouble. First it blew warm and then cold and it kept me busy every minute.

"You ought to have seen that crowd in Buffalo at the driving park. It was one of the biggest that I have ever seen. It seemed to me there was a square mile of people and there was not a person to bother me when I started."

Arrangements had been made by the Carnival committee to store the machine in a tent on the triangle off

Riverway. The question of how to get the delicate mechanical bird to the quarters provided was a difficult one. Finally it was decided to tow it through the streets. Under the watchful eyes of Beachey, his mechanician and business manager, willing hands were ready to tackle the job. A squad of blue coats was finally selected, and followed by hundred of curious spectators, the march was commenced. Only a short distance had been transversed when the storm broke, and a rush for shelter was necessary. Beachey's party and the patrolmen "stood by their guns" and received a drenching.

Later when the skies cleared a triumphal entry into the business part of the city was made, and the vast crowd that lined the sidewalks had an opportunity to see the aeroplane at close range.[4]

At the Carnival, Harry Houdini's tightrope walk across the gorge was canceled because of legal complications regarding the USA/Canada border. Bobby Leech went over the Falls in a barrel, but was caught in the turbulence below for three hours, breaking both of his knees. The leaders of the Carnival committee came to Lincoln Beachey to save the event. He was to receive $4000 to fly through the gorge; they offered an extra $1000 in gold if he could fly under the Honeymoon bridge as well.

The following morning, the last day of the Carnival, arrived with blustery winds and rain. Canadian and American military gave simultaneous 21-gun salutes from both sides of the Falls. Then they joined forces for a grand military parade, "an international display of friendship by thousands of troops under arms," as 2,000 homing pigeons were released. Despite the inclement weather, *a quarter of a million people* showed up in the hope of seeing an aeroplane dare the mighty Falls. Late that afternoon, Lincoln's plane was towed to the open field at Ninth and Niagara. Hundreds of people swarmed into the area, where dozens of police had to hold them back.[5]

Lincoln could feel it. The sense of mortality pressed darkly upon him like the boiling sky. He pushed away his doubts and fears and the promised glory as well, and became so concentrated on his task he even forgot the vast crowds. He had felt their excitement, their marvelous and morbid fascination. He despised seeing the betting pools form, money changing hands everywhere, where the daily odds were 5-to-1 that he would not live out the day. Today, he overheard 20-to-1. He remembered the crowds tearing apart fallen birdmen. Yes, the people had come to see the new flying machine, but he also knew they had come to see him die.

Lincoln knew if he postponed the feat, there would be widespread gossip that he was a fake. But he felt it could be done—just like the Fillmore hill. His new 'trick,' the vertical drop or "the dip of death" or "a Beachey" as the newspapers called it, gave his sturdy Curtiss Pusher tremendous control and stability at the bottom of the drop, even in blustery conditions. He would plummet into the canyon from on high, gaining tremendous speed, just as he had done on his bike into Cow Hollow. The swirling winds of Horseshoe Falls would be the major challenge, but if he survived the Falls, the canyon and Honeymoon Bridge would be easy.

Beachey turned to the Fair's manager: "Mr. Worthington, tell them I am going to go for the bridge as well."

The sound of the announcement went through the ocean of people like a wave across water. Scant few in the vast crowd had ever seen a winged flying machine before, though most knew the name of Lincoln Beachey from his dirigible days as the boy-wonder aeronaut. Crowds filled the canyon around the falls, filled the bridges, and filled the streets of both cities of Niagara where a view could be had.

The mechanic turned the propeller on the Curtiss Pusher and the power-plant exploded into life. With the motor behind the wings and the pilot way out front, the craft was perfect for vision, deadly for mistakes. Though climbing out of the city park would not have been easy even in a calm wind, Lincoln bolted into the air to the cheering of thousands.

Flight over Niagara Falls, June 26, 1911

Beachey goes airborne from the open field at Ninth and Niagara.

Beachey heads towards Canada and Horseshoe Falls.

Several steam engines from the Erie and New York Central Railroads saluted with their whistles, and the Maid of the Mist tourist boats followed suit, ringing their bells as Lincoln climbed high behind Horseshoe Falls. One last turn upward and, at 1500 feet, Beachey prepared to dive. From his vantage point he could see downstream and the water thundering over the edge of the precipice, creating clouds of rising mist.

"Like a hawk diving for its prey,"[6] Lincoln dropped out of the sky, headed for the edge in the middle of Horseshoe Falls. As he came to the top of the Falls, he unbelievably *disappeared* into the rising vapor of the deadly cataract! Above on the canyon's edge, parents covered their children's eyes and women "fainted by the thousands". The first aeroplane they had ever seen had vanished into the mist! Screams of horror filled the air. Another fool, it appeared, had sacrificed his life to the waters of the mighty Falls.

As Lincoln entered the mist, the spray stung his face so badly he had to close his eyes. He pulled back on his controls with all of his power and, without his sight, prayed that his timing was right.

"Shooting out like a cannonball" from the bottom of the mist, Lincoln Beachey struggled with the whirling winds. His motor had sucked in too much water and began to sputter and die. With no power to fight the swirling winds, Beachey prepared to hit the river. Within inches of the water and seconds of disaster, his motor gracefully kicked back in. Steadily gaining power and control, Beachey headed for the arch of Honeymoon Bridge. He had made it thus far and was going for the bonus of $1000 in gold.

The crowds erupted in roaring cheers. Lincoln passed under the Honeymoon girders, then suddenly turned his Curtiss skyward and passed <u>over</u> the next bridge, missing it by only a few feet!

People cheered, boats and trains tooted. At the landing field Canada's Mayor Dores of Niagara, Manager Worthington, and scores of photographers and reporters waited. This was one landing Lincoln dearly relished.

"It was the most exciting trip of my life," said Beachey after he had landed safely. "I shut my eyes as I flew toward the arch, for into my face the spray cloud of the waterfall was driven as I descended into the gorge. I was fearful that I might strike, but they tell me I took it in a beautiful manner. I am glad not to have disappointed such an appreciative crowd."

Close to the edge... Beachey's feat of going over Horseshoe Falls inspired artists and advertisements for decades.

At Niagara Falls, Lincoln Beachey flies over the Maid of the Mist boat and heads under Honeymoon Bridge. *Courtesy City of Niagara Archives*

Crowds lined the Honeymoon Bridge at Niagara, watching Beachey swoop out
of the mist, down the river gorge, and under the bridge.
Courtesy City of Niagara Archives

That evening, riding in an open car through the streets of both Niagaras, Lincoln bathed in glory such as he had never received before. "One hundred newspapers declared him the eighth wonder of the world, and his dive into the Falls the greatest aerial feat all time."[7] He had not died, and to the throngs appeared immortal. The parade ended with a celebration at the Imperial Hotel where dignitaries and reporters had the opportunity to talk with the intrepid Californian. Lincoln felt comfortable: he had imagined this moment before, and glory felt like an old dream come true.

Amidst reverence usually reserved for Olympian champions in their own town, Lincoln received praise, acclaim, and his $5000. Champagne flowed freely as everyone wanted to talk to and be seen talking to a world-famous hero.

Because of Beachey's Niagara spectacular, plain flying was suddenly passé. Aviation's exhibition era came to an abrupt, if marvelous, end. The tea leaves could be read. "With all due respect to Glenn Curtiss, the Wrights and other pioneers whose achievements will ever be remembered, the ordinary aeroplane flights such as they now give, even with the new hydroplane device, no longer satisfy the public. And this is no compliment to the public, either. Recent events are demonstrating that the people want thrillers and, in plain terms, this means an extreme risking of human life. The ordinary flights have become so common as no longer to attract crowds."

Notes

1. *San Francisco Examiner*, January 1911.
2. *Chicago Tribune*, June 13, 1965.
3. Hillery Beachey Collection, San Diego Aerospace Museum.
4. *Cataract Journal*, June 26, 1911.
5. and 6. Articles from the *Cataract Journal* and the *Niagara Falls Gazette*, June 27, 1911.
7. *Rochester Herald*, June 29, 1911.

THE CHICAGO DAILY TRIBUNE, SATURDAY, AUGUST 12 1911

Famous Aviators Who Will Do Stunts in the Air at Chicago Meet.

Excitement was high in Chicago as the city prepared to welcome aviators from all over the world in 1911. At top center are Beachey, left, and Eugen Ely, with English pilot Thomas Sopwith at their right; Glenn Curtiss, bottom left row. Captain Thomas Baldwin is second from right in the second row. At bottom right is Cal Rodgers, the first man to fly across the U.S. Rodgers and Ely both eventually died imitating Beachey's maneuvers. *Courtesy San Diego Aerospace Museum*

The Greatest Aviation Meet of All Time

S ix weeks later, rolling into Chicago, Lincoln felt anxious. This was not the kind of fear against which you measure your skill—the kind that is conquered with endless practice. This was different.

During the eight months since he first fell with his motor off, Lincoln had practiced longer and steeper drops, intentionally allowing his machine to stall and whirl toward the ground, recovering just in time. Learning to beat the spiral drop gave Lincoln great confidence. He shook off the fear he felt and concentrated instead on defending his unofficial title as the best flyer in the land.

The top thirty-two aviators from all over the world were meeting in Chicago, August 12 through August 20, 1911, to compete for $100,000 in prize money. Lincoln would not be the only flyer in the sky to be adored, and he knew the limitations of the high-powered Curtiss biplane would eliminate him from many contests based on altitude and distance. To emerge the champion, he would have to win most of the races and accuracy events. Thomas Octave Sopwith, one year younger than Lincoln and already acclaimed, was coming from England with his new monoplane—lighter, with a motor as renown as a Curtiss. He'd be tough. Cal Rodgers was to fly the Wright brothers'

This "doctored" picture, made for the Chicago Meet, shows a flock of flying machines hovering over Michigan Avenue, with the train tracks and Grant Park at right. Beachey is second from left in the bottom row. *Author's private collection*

latest machine. One thing Lincoln did not want: to be laughed at as he had been at Dominguez when he was outflown by a lighter, more advanced machine.

Regardless of who got the largest share of the $100,000 dollar prize, Beachey was determined to give the best performances. That kind of money was attracting the world's very best, and the crowds promised to be as large as Niagara's. This would be the greatest aviation meet of all time, a world stage. Lincoln was beginning to be known as *the* best, but now he had to prove it.

Back at the hotel, Lincoln met the newest member of the team, Blanche Scott. This woman had created quite a stir. She was the first woman to drive across the country in a car, and was said to be as fine a mechanician as you could find. And now she was flying. She didn't have to do anything but plain, simple flying to get the crowd to swoon. "Pleased to meet you, Miss Scott. I'm so glad you're here on the Curtiss

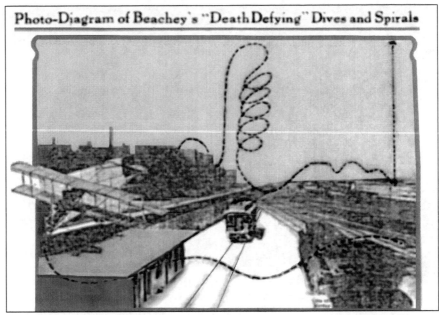

Photo-Diagram of Beachey's "Death Defying" Dives and Spirals

Newspaper illustrators had to use ingenuity to show readers what Beachey's student were like, since no one had ever seen such maneuvers before. He literally danced his wheels across the tops to the rail cars. *Courtesy Glenn Curtiss Museum*

team. Welcome aboard. You know, I've been training a female flyer myself," said Lincoln.

Lincoln looked toward his traveling partners and gave them a wink, then back at Blanche and the rest of the team. "Yes, a French girl," Lincoln continued. "She's a sweet girl, but this is just business, I assure you." Then turning to Curtiss. "I could send for her if you want. We could enter her as a novice."

Blanche Scott frowned at Lincoln. But Pickens, Curtiss' new promoter, enthusiastically encouraged the idea. "Yessiree! Bring her. We can prove that aeroplanes are for everybody, and boost our sales."

Glenn Curtiss consented, to the delight of both his promoter and his number one pilot, but he wondered how news of this lady had escaped him. "How come I didn't know about this? What's her name?"

The question caught Lincoln by surprise. "Uh, Mademoiselle, uh Clarice Lavaseur. Met her in Philadelphia and gave her a few lessons."

Beachey's first attempt at flying in drag was his outrageous performance as Madame Lavaseur in Chicago. It was not his last. *Courtesy San Diego Aerospace Museum*

Someone snickered and Lincoln went on: "No, really, I'm sure she'll surprise you, in fact, that's why you don't know; I wanted to surprise you." Lincoln knew he had pulled it off.

Suddenly two men approached the group. The first one asked, "Mister Glenn Hammond Curtiss?" and when Glenn nodded, handed him some papers and pronounced, "You are being sued by the Wright Company for patent violation. We have filed an injunction to stop this meet and prohibit anyone from flying unless they agree to licensing and percentages."

The Curtiss team was shocked by the intrusion. But then the second gentleman stepped forward and handed Curtiss more papers. His voice was firm, but gentle. "Don't worry fellas, they are suing everybody. We are backing you 100%. Here's a letter from the general manager explaining the situation with the Wrights."

The general manager of the meet publicly accused the Wrights: "they want the certainty of receiving more money from the meet than anybody else," he said. The Association announced that the event would be open and competitive, and that "it would make 'common cause' with any flyers who might be harassed by the Wrights' legal proceedings." George Guy, secretary of the New York Electrical Society, wrote the Association to convey his encouragement to Cyrus McCormick, the organizer and treasurer of the meet. "The whole country will hail you as the deliverers of aviation from the greedy grip of the Wrights." The eyes of the nation would be on this great event.

Lincoln was more determined than ever to take Chicago.

At the approach to Grant Park, banners welcomed the crowds and advised expedient ways to enter and pay. Grandstand seats were 50¢, $1, and $1.50; box seats were $2, standing room a quarter, children ten cents. Everything was sold out. Near the park itself, it was almost impossible to move in any direction. People stood in the streets, on bridges, on rooftops; children climbed lamp poles and hung from trees. By the time Lincoln entered the fast climb event, the crowd had swelled to 600,000, a throng of historic record, all waiting for something marvelous to happen.

Beachey would not disappoint them. Thomas Sopwith had set the standard with his new high-powered

Postcard of Beachey setting new flying records.

monoplane, and Lincoln knew he would have to push his climb to the limit. As he watched his altimeter hit the three thousand foot mark, he looked at his stopwatch. Just behind Sopwith. He looked down at the throngs and he arched his machine into a wild plummeting spiral toward the train tracks that ran along the lakeside. The cross-bracing between his wings gave the plane great strength, and Lincoln knew they could take the force as he pulled up sharply from his steep dive.

No one could accuse Lincoln Beachey of being under-dressed for his performances. His natty chalk-striped suit, white shirt and tie helped him to convey the
idea that flying planes was a perfectly normal occupation.

Courtesy San Diego Aerospace Museum

Pushing the plane to its limits as he recovered, his vision narrowed
and became spotty as the blood left his head from the g-force. Lincoln
knew how to walk that line.

Lincoln picked a locomotive lumbering into downtown and dropped
along the side of the passenger cars, waving at the shocked riders, then
bolted up and over to the other side, waving to the shocked passengers on that side as well. Finally, he danced his wheels across the tops of
the train cars, hopping from one car to the next.[1] People in the crowd
gasped and screamed and applauded wildly. Beachey finally set his flying
machine down in front of the grandstand, and the crowd erupted. He

may have come in second in the fast climb, but the crowd was his. He bowed, he basked in their adoration, and he forgot about everything else.

Beachey's drag performances were enormously popular with his fans.
Courtesy San Diego Aerospace Museum

The weekday crowds were estimated to be 100,000, but they swelled noticeably when Lincoln Beachey was scheduled to fly. Another draw was Lincoln Beachey's student, Madam Clarice Lavaseur, flying Beachey's own aeroplane in the novice category. Beachey had rigged his plane to give him lateral, aileron control from his movable seat, using his torso; he also had grown proficient in moving his rudder controls back and forth with only his knees. He was ready for hands-free flying.

When the novice exhibitions commenced, Clarice, overdressed in the latest French fashion, waddled onto the field and delicately straddled the pilot's seat. She pulled her skirt down to cover her revealed pink undergarments and the ladies in the crowd blushed and ooo-ed in sympathy for her. She tucked in her long auburn hair, adjusted her embroidered vest, and set her boot heels upon the footrest. The propeller was spun, the motor began to roar, and the young French girl headed the aeroplane across the field. Suddenly she pulled upwards into the air, too steeply, and stalled. She fell forward, regaining partial control only at the last possible instant, her wheels skipping across the hard earth. Up and down she roller-coastered, gathering speed and momentum, finally gaining some control. She flew out beyond the tracks and was circling back towards the grandstand when her skirt suddenly blew over her face. Clarice grabbed frantically for the fabric, taking her hands away from the hand controls, and began screaming, "HELP!!!"

It was the crowd's worst nightmare: a flying machine was out of control and headed directly toward them. There was pandemonium as hundreds of spectators scattered, ducked, and prayed for their very lives. Miraculously, the machine pulled up only eight feet from disaster, and poor Mademoiselle Lavaseur and the flying machine went screaming out of the Park, as she kept trying to tear her dress away from her face.

Emergency crews raced after the plane. Telephone operators spread the electric news: a flying machine, out of control, was headed for downtown Chicago, piloted by a hysterical woman.

Entering Michigan Avenue, the plane continued flying erratically. Madam Lavaseur danced her tricycle undercarriage across the cobblestones, one wheel, then another, as she chased cars and wagons onto the sidewalks. Cars unable to get out of the way were used as launching ramps as Clarice pulled up from the street and rolled her wheels across the tops of several automobiles.[2]

Madam Lavaseur navigated the canyons of downtown, ducked under power lines, skated the plane's wheels across streets, cars, and buildings, and finally emerged high above the metropolitan area. Below, Cal Rodgers flew by, and suddenly Clarice lost control again and dived at the Wright machine, rolling her plane's wheels across Cal's wings. Rodgers panicked, and dumped his plane in Lake Michigan.

Madam Clarice Lavaseur again seemed to have no control as her machine plummeted toward a ferry below filled with people watching the airshow. The passengers jumped en masse into the cool summer waters. The aviatrix pulled her machine up just in the nick of time, coasted across the train tracks and set the flying machine down with grace in front of the grandstand.

The crowd broke into applause. Madam Lavaseur stepped down from her machine and curtseyed politely again and again. Then, as she took a long deep bow, she removed her wig, revealing the rich auburn hair of the incomparable Lincoln Beachey. The crowds laughed, sent up three cheers, and continued a ten-minute ovation.

"I knew it was him all along," became the common lie. Lincoln Beachey had won the hearts of the people of Chicago, but he was fined several hundred dollars for his near miss of the crowds and his mid-air kiss of Cal Rodgers.[3]

Beachey could hardly stand it when other aviators wowed the crowds with tricks he had long since mastered. When the Frenchman Rene Simon waved bye to Beachey at 4500 feet to dash back to earth, Lincoln punctuated his skill by waiting and waiting. When Simon had descended all the way down to 1000 feet, Beachey spiraled straight at the ground and landed his machine while the Frenchman was still 500 feet up! A vast sigh went up from the crowd when Beachey lightly touched down, because every single person had thought the machine was out of control. The aviation experts, still under the illusion that the spiral glide was a death sentence declared Beachey's skills were unequaled in the history of air sport. Beachey had to engage lengthy debates with newspapermen, "in an attempt to prove that the spiral glide [spin] as he does it is not necessarily dangerous."

Early the next day, an American flyer, William Badger, also eager to impress the crowds, tried to imitate Lincoln's vertical drop, but at the bottom of the dive his wings collapsed, and he fell like a rock to his death. Another pilot, who became transfixed watching Badger's fatal crash from the air, lost control of his machine and also plunged to his demise. Unfortunately for Lincoln, the media linked the deaths to 'doing a Beachey,' as they called his vertical drop. A long series imitators would meet the same gruesome fate.

INTERNATIONAL
AVIATION MEET
AT GRANT PARK,
CHICAGO,
AUGUST 12–20,
1911

C. P. Rodgers flying over
boats in Lake Michigan

The Most Prominent Aviators of the day, 1911.

Planes flying over the crowd
at Grant Park, Chicago, 1911

Beachey at Chicago Meet, Aug. 12-20, 1911

Beachey ready
to take off

International Aviation Meet Grant Park Chicago August 12-20, 1911

Price 25 Cents

Official Souvenir Program

Wreck of McCurdy's biplane, 1911

Blanche Stewart Scott was the
only woman to be taught to fly
by Glenn Curtiss.

The day following the fatalities vast crowds jammed the aviation field—and equally packed to suffocation were the nearby streets, parking spaces, and bleachers erected on roofs of high-rise buildings surrounding the event —"in the morbid hope that the spectacular accidents of Tuesday would be repeated."

Chicago reporters exuded. "On previous days they had come to see mechanical contrivances shooting through the air. On Wednesday they came to see live men, daring young aviators, hurtling to their death through space. They were disappointed, for only once did they rise to their feet and utter groans—half delight, half horror—as Lincoln Beachey shot from a height of nearly 3,000 feet and seemed to be rushing to his death with the speed of an express train.

Then when he settled easily with the wind a few feet above the ground and landed gracefully, cheer after cheer rang out. Exclamations of relief and sighs of satisfaction were heard on all sides. Every one was pleased, having witnessed a man shooting to earth and experienced all the thrills of a great catastrophe without the toll of human life."

Thomas Sopwith's monoplane impressed Lincoln. It climbed 1,634 feet in three minutes, a world record. Sopwith was ahead of him in winnings, but his monoplane could not take the stress of dives, as the Curtiss biplane could. Both aviators had over ten thousand dollars of the prize money, but Sopwith was clearly ahead of Beachey in winnings. On the last day of the Chicago meet, only the altitude contest remained. Lincoln desperately wanted to add to his total and finish strong in second-place winnings. But Curtiss machines were designed for power, speed, and maneuverability—not distance, not altitude.

Lincoln quizzed the Curtiss engineers about the possibility of winning the altitude contest. They explained that it was a simple matter of consumption and efficiency. "You see Lincoln, it has to do with how much fuel it takes to get one of our machines up there and back again. A Wright contraption will probably win it because that's where the low-powered, large winged machines excel."

Suddenly Beachey blurted, "That's it!" and swung into action.

He ordered Pickens, Curtiss' promoter, to enter him into the altitude event, and hustled the mechanicians to prepare his machine.

Lincoln poured the gasoline himself, filling the tank to the last drop, wiping the overflow from the tank with his own handkerchief. As he sat down and belted himself in, an engineer shrieked unknowingly, "What do you mean 'that's it'?" It was obvious to Lincoln. He replied, "Who needs gas to get back down?"[4]

The motor was kicked on, and Lincoln's only adjustment to his attire was to turn the brim of his hat to the rear. It was his own personal signal to the crowds that the show was about to begin, and as always, when he spun his hat, the legions bellowed.

Beachey tops off his motor with gasoline to go higher than anyone ever before.

Over the hour and forty-eight minutes of skillful climbing, the roar of the mighty machine became a faint buzz. Then the tiny speck above the clouds sputtered and went silent. With the whole sky as his playground, Lincoln Beachey swooped and swirled, like a seagull dancing in infinite space. For twelve glorious minutes he fell across the sky, diving, turning, spinning, and when he touched down with silent grace, everyone else found out what he already knew. The world record for altitude had been shattered, 11, 642 feet, in a stocky Curtiss, by Lincoln Beachey, of course. [5]

Notes

1. Personal Interview: Early Bird Forest Wysong, who attended the Chicago meet as a novice aviator.
2. Ibid.
3. *Chicago Daily Tribune*, August 14, 1911.
4. Don Dwiggins, *The Air Devils*, "California Flying Fool," p. 88.
5. Ibid.

Glenn Curtiss and Lincoln Beachey, the two most famous aviators in America,
met in Hammondsport in 1912 to discuss plane design.

Courtesy Glenn Curtiss Museum

Rare photos of May Beachey, seated in the front of Beachey's
motorcycle built for two (left), and in her husband's plane seat (right).

Courtesy San Francisco Motorcycle Club (left)

"I Am Not Crazy!"

Throughout 1912, American interest in aviation was fueled by exhibitions held all over the country. Wilbur Wright died of typhoid fever in May, and flyers everywhere expressed the hope that the Wrights' lawsuit would be dropped. On the contrary, Orville and his sister Katherine blamed Glenn Curtiss for the illness that struck down their brother, and Orville was even more determined to win his patent suit against Curtiss and other flyers. It was the Wrights vs. the world. The U.S. government felt it could not invest heavily in aviation until the courts had resolved the issue, and was thus the most crippled in terms of air power.

Lincoln toured constantly, consumed with expanding the capability of the aeroplane and bringing aviation to the masses. "I'm learning new things each day, and my flying is an education to all. The thrills are merely thrown in to attract the people, much in the same way that good music draws people to lectures and other educational affairs. But man has conquered the sky, just as he mastered the earth and water, and as we get further along, we will find safety in the air we cannot find on the land or on the water. Listen on Monday to the unbeliever of Saturday. After they have seen me, they will know that the aeroplane is not an experimental flying machine any more."[1]

Beachey and a co-pilot test Curtiss' latest invention, a hydroplane, on Lake Kekua, at Hammondsport. Curtiss, wearing white shoes, is at right.
Courtesy Hud Weeks Collection

Still, every performance spawned large betting pools, with the odds always against Lincoln Beachey living out the day. Every month, some-times every week, the press reported another flyer had died 'trying to do a Beachey,' whether it was true or not. And with every death, the crowds grew larger. Instead of coming to see the 'Master Birdman' fly, they came to see him die. He was called crazy, a fool who had been lucky.

Lincoln could not believe how poorly he was appreciated. The crowds were vast, but did not recognize what was truly before them. Lincoln wanted them to understand he was not crazy or a daredevil, but was the pioneer of a new art and science. Neither the crowds nor many other aviators acknowledged his endless practice: either they called him crazy or they died trying to imitate him.

When Lincoln was asked to speak to the Boy Scouts after an ex-hibition, he said, "I want to impress upon you that I am not endowed with supernatural powers, that I am not superhuman in any respect.

The things I accomplished in the air have been the outgrowth of constant practice, of gradual learning and evolution. I would not make a straight descent or a spiral or anything the first time. It was merely by means of gradual working into them that the feats that I am able to accomplish were made possible. What I have been able to learn in aviation by means of a slow process is possible in any other field of endeavor and I want to caution you boys to make haste slowly, in whatever line you take up. Keep plugging away at it, learn by degrees and you can accomplish almost anything."[2]

In addition to his regular displays of aerial artistry, Lincoln would often race his plane against big name automobile drivers, most notably the legendary Barney Oldfield and "Crazy Eddie" Rickenbacker. Lincoln would have to keep his airplane low and inside the track to please the crowds, and he almost always won the contests. He repeatedly urged Eddie to take up flying, so impressed was he with the way Rickenbacker handled a machine at high speeds. Racing against ground speedsters provided Lincoln with an electrifying stage to demonstrate his absolute control, even though they continued to call both Lincoln and Eddie "crazy".

Two articles speak colorfully about the crowds' fascination with aviation and its greatest performer.

AERIAL TRICKS ALARM CROWD

Los Angeles' International Aviation meet opened promptly at 2:30 o'clock. Kearney took off and climbed into the sky. Beachey began his hair-raising stunts right away, doing the "ocean roll" [quick rolls 180 degrees one way and then the other creating a long, wave-like pattern] right in front of the grandstand, with the wheels of his machine not being more than two feet from the earth.

Suddenly Beachey and Kearney started their brother

act. The crowd held its breath as the two biplanes nearly collided in the air and then began circling around each other, and dipping under and over each other — sort of a game of leapfrog in the air. It was an amazing feat in aerial vaudeville. At frequent intervals the wings of the two machines almost touched and at no time were they more than a few feet apart.

The nerve-racking spectacle was too much for William H. Pickens, the official starter, and he waved a white flag as a signal to turn their attention to some less dangerous form of amusement. A sigh of relief went up when the biplanes separated.

After this Beachey went through with an aerial turkey trot in front of the grandstand, which was scarcely less thrilling than the brother act. Part of the time he flew with hands off the steering wheel and controls. Before finally landing Kearney and Beachey both made a graceful spiral curve downwards.

A more exciting race was never seen than the one between Beachey and the auto racer Barney Oldfield. The birdman won easily, but it was his terrifying feats while over the head of the man in the auto that furnished the thrills. He seemed trying to skim Oldfield's head with the rear wheels of his machine and once there was not more than two inches of space between him and his object. Several times the automobilist was forced to duck to escape being touched. First the flyer would race beside him, the wheels of his biplane barely off the ground, then he would leap-frog over the car, then soar into the air and go through some skillful evolutions and a moment later would be on the straightway to make up lost time. The birdman won narrowly.

Before coming to the ground Beachey performed several more of his tricks, including the ocean roll, and the

Texas Tommy which Lincoln does by touching one wheel to the ground and then the other, dancing back and forth. Finally his reverse spiral was the ultimate thriller.

INTO THE CLOUDS

At 3:45 o'clock Beachey was again in the air and this time he performed with his hands off the steering wheel and levers most of the tricks other flyers perform with both hands and feet on the controls. He flew for twelve minutes in this fashion. At the end of twelve minutes he started to climb in preparation for his dive. He attained an altitude of 3500 feet, then shut off his motor and shot in a perpendicular line for the earth. A hush fell over the throng. The sound of wind passing through the wire stays of the biplane could be heard in every part of the enclosure. In a few seconds it was over. The machine tilted upward suddenly and landed with the grace of a gull.[3]

In the summer of 1912, the *Omaha Gazette* covered the amusing story of Nebraska's Native Americans and their first encounter with an aeroplane, revealing the narrow prejudices of the times, as well as the mutual respect between the Native Americans and "The Man Who Flew with the Eagles."

INDIANS INSPECT BEACHEY'S CRAFT

West met East, the man of yesterday clasped hands with the man of tomorrow, at the State Fair grounds this morning, when Running Hawk and twenty-five of his braves visited the famous aviator and his flying machine with which he performs apparently impossible feats and puts to shame all laws of gravitation.

The Sioux Indians, who form a portion of the Inhabitants of the village from the Pine Ridge agency that is on the grounds, were in charge with their superintendent, Charles Eason, their interpreter.

Fully equipped with headdresses, ornaments, fringed leggings and all other finery of the redman, their faces streaked with paint, the twenty five braves crowded about the delicate machine that carries Lincoln Beachey onto cloudland. Astonishment of the power of the motor marked the visit of the Sioux.

"This motor has the power of eighty ponies," the interpreter told them.

WOULDN'T BELIEVE IT

The statement was met with negative shakes of the head and derisive laughter on the part of the Indians. They refused to believe that in so small a machine the power of eighty ponies was herded.

When the aviator himself was introduced to the aborigines, the interpreter was flooded with compliments on the airman's bravery that each individual wished to pay. Beachey returned the compliments by telling the interpreter his opinion of the high standard of bravery manifested by the Indian tribes.

After a considerable visit in which Beachey and his mechanicians tried to explain the workings of the aeroplane, the Indians returned to their quarters, thoroughly inspired with a wholesome respect for the science of white man in general and for the bravery of one particular paleface.[4]

ALBUQUERQUE MC

THIRTY-FOURTH YEAR, VOL. CLXXVI, No. 8.   ALBUQUERQUE, NEW MEXICO

LINCOLN BEACHEY PROVES HE IS WORLD'S GREATEST BIRDMAN

AVIATOR ELECTRIFIES CROWDS BY HIS DEATH DEFYING STUNTS PERFORMED IN FIRST DAY'S FLIGHTS

Information Bureau Taking Care of Room Hunters

WITH HANDS OFF LEVERS AND BODY SWAYING HE GLIDES, DIPS AND

Lincoln has begun to lose his boyish look, and has traded his traditional tweed cap for a corduroy one. On his shoulders are leather straps, the first restraints he used other than a seat belt. *Courtesy San Diego Aerospace Museum*

Beachey confers with his mechanician and Roy Knabenshue (right), before a performance. *Courtesy San Diego Aerospace Museum*

But neither Beachey's insistence on his seriousness nor the praise of Native Americans would squelch the fire of public misunderstanding. The crowds seemed only bloodthirsty, and every day's betting pool offered heavy odds against his living out the day. Lincoln reacted at the money exchanges happening right in front of him and cynically snarled at a reporter, "Art and science? Bah! Forget all that kind of talk. It is the dull thud of dollars as they bounce in the strongbox that lures me to continue. Get me right, I am no fool. I am simply Beachey, the man who digs gold out of the sky."[5]

He was called the Master Birdman, but to the crowds he seemed crazy. Lincoln suffered the genius's misunderstanding. Everywhere he traveled in the summer of 1912, people came in droves, expecting—even hoping—to see him die. No wonder he personally inspected his craft in detail before each flight.

ack in California, Lincoln looked forward to a performance at the
state capitol. The governor would understand him. Hiram Johnson
was an intelligent man. Sacramento would be good, Lincoln hoped.
The rising tide of bad publicity over the deaths of Beachey imitators
would be stemmed. He would make people understand aerobatics was
a science and art—and the imitators were foolhardy in their rushed
attempts to duplicate his feats.

Lincoln put on a dazzling show for Governor Johnson. The governor and his wife bounded from their box seat to meet the twenty-
five-year-old Beachey. Johnson's hand extended to shake Lincoln's, "We
thought for sure you were going to die," blurted the governor. He did
not realize that he had not praised Lincoln but insulted him.

Legend has it that Lincoln, boiling with frustration, left the governor's hand empty hanging and instead snatched the lace handkerchief
from clasped hands of Mrs. Johnson.

Beachey in Curtiss biplane.

The large motor with its clumsy square radiator, the large, backward facing propeller, and the pilot far outweighs the fragile frame of the aircraft.

Lincoln marched to the middle of the field and dropped the handkerchief onto the grass. He climbed aboard his machine, ordered the motor to be started, took off, and roared up and up and up. At three thousand feet he killed his motor and let his machine fall into a vertical drop. When the wires began to scream, he spun his machine as well, the 'Beachey bore'—with the handkerchief as the bull's eye. Everyone jumped to their feet to see Lincoln not only pull out of the dive of death, but pick up the handkerchief with his wing tip!

The crowd fell back in stunned disbelief. But Lincoln was not through. He pointed his machine for the governor's box and as he passed, his coat fluttered down. Beachey circled and another piece of clothing fell. He continued in this way, circling and disrobing, until he was wearing only his long underwear. He landed in front of his hanger, jumped out of his seat onto the ground, struck a pose in the afternoon sunlight, and remarked, "Now I'd like to know what that stuffed shirt has to say about Lincoln Beachey."[6]

In his desperate attempt to show absolute mastery of the aeroplane, Beachey pushed his demonstration to the limit—often perpetuating the very illusion of being crazy that he was trying to dispel. According to Bert Dudek and Col. H.C. Adamson, Beachey scared the dickens out of a roller coaster full of youngsters in Cincinnati. Walking through an amusement park where he was scheduled to fly, Beachey remarked he would like to ride the roller coaster sometime. That very day, at his customary three o'clock, he went aloft, and flying about 600 feet, he spied a car full of merrymakers on the roller coaster. As they came up to the top of an incline and slowed before they zoomed down, Beachey flew directly over the rear car and proceeded to follow the coaster point blank, taking the turns and dips the car took. The youngsters in the car were frantic and ran to their parents in tears, but they later forgave Beachey when he gave each of them his autograph and photographs.

Lincoln insisted that his shows be a 3 o'clock for a specific reason: for the children would just be out of school and could come. They weren't unbelievers; the children would be the future he was showing them.

Lincoln persistently berated the federal government for not doing more for aviation; pushing the lawmakers beyond their inaction was a deep passion for him. The Europeans were rushing headlong into aero-development, and even Mexico had a larger air force than America did. Lincoln repeatedly asked to show the Army what the aeroplane could really do, until finally, publicly pressured, the air training personnel at College Park, Maryland, consented to let the 'stuntman' give them instruction.

Beachey was too eager to amaze the young cadets on the simplicity and safety of the aeroplane. At College Park, "Beachey demonstrated flight without the use of a rudder. Using one of the Army planes, he had the rudder removed and went aloft, making three figure-eights, and landed within a 600 square foot area, which was marked off with flags. He went aloft again with the rudder re-attached and really gave the plane a work-out. He then 'buzzed" the hangers, making the authorities frantic."[7]

Colonel Hans Christian Adamson (appointed by five-star General Hap Arnold himself to record the history of the Air Force upon its inception in the 1940s) tells us that Beachey enraged the commander but inspired a lieutenant.

The bombing run looked spectacular to everyone watching from the outside of the operations cabin, but on the inside, Captain Charles Chandler was banging both fists on his desk.

Hap Arnold

"Hap, is that an Army plane?" the captain demanded angrily.

Lieutenant Hap Arnold had been watching spellbound from the window. He nodded proudly, "Yes, sir. One of our new Curtiss-Ds."

"Who in the hell is flying it? . . . Never mind! It's Beachey, isn't it? Why is he flying so damn close to the building? He's here to teach our men how to operate these new machines, not to show off his latest stunts!"

"Those aren't tricks, captain. He's demonstrating incredible control. Why, I never imagined an aeroplane could make such maneuvers. I really think we should go outside, sir, to get a better look."

Lieutenant Arnold and the enraged officer stepped outside just in time to see Lincoln buzzing a column of marching soldiers. The officers in front waved frantically, but the pilot did not respond. As Lincoln lowered his aeroplane to within inches of their heads, the soldiers dropped to the ground. The captain was infuriated.

"Who does he think he is? Those men could have been killed! I thought something like this might happen. Beachey's so damn full of his own reputation that he thinks he can get away with everything! Well, he's wrong. This is the Army, not a circus! I want you to issue an order effective immediately, forbidding him to fly Army planes at this field!"

But Arnold had seen much more in Lincoln's demonstration than a circus act. "But, sir, he's here at our invitation," he protested. "He's considered the top aviator in the world, and he's certainly showing us the real power of the Curtiss motor and the kinds of maneuvers our own new machines are capable of."

The enraged captain snapped back. "Maneuvers, I'll say! If our men try and imitate that lunatic, soon we won't have any pilots— they'll all be dead!"

But sir—"

"That's an order, Lieutenant!"

Later, Lincoln protested the Captain's order. "Military flying will not likely be a tame affair. The pilot of the future must be a skilled craftsman, ready to perform under extreme conditions. I do not mean to 'tickle fate under the chin', or do anything that endangers my life, but I am simply not content with straight flying. You can assure your captain that I know what I'm doing all the time, Lieutenant. There is no danger in my stunts. I do not see what all this fuss is about, for it is my own business if I drop a few hundred feet, and I've certainly got enough in the bank to take care of the undertaker's bills. Anytime I have to let anyone dictate to me about my flying, then I am through."

The lieutenant confessed, "Mr. Beachey, after seeing your demonstration today, I have been awakened to the limitless wonder of the aviation. In your hands the aeroplane is no longer an unwieldy kite, but rather a rival to the birds themselves."[8]

Even though the lieutenant pledged his undying support to the aeroplane program, Capt. Chandler banned Beachey not only from that Army base, but from all Army bases. By year's end, Lincoln's whole world seemed to be coming apart. His friend and teammate, Eugene Ely, who had begun Naval aviation in San Francisco, fell to his death in Georgia, 'trying to do a Beachey' for his taunting wife. Lincoln received a letter from Mrs. Ely, which read, "God punish you Lincoln Beachey. Gene would be with me now if he had not seen you fly."[9] Lincoln could not believe her: it was her prodding and nagging that killed him. Still, Lincoln felt as if he had been kicked in the chest, and he was not happy.

Lincoln retreated to Hammondsport and together with Curtiss began an altogether new design: instead of a pusher design where the pilot sat out front, the engine was out front, pulling-"tractor" style, and the pilot sat behind. *This plane was the forerunner of the Jenny airplane of WWI*, described by Curtiss as the Beachey Tractor. A press release sent by telegram in late 1912 announced the new machine to the world:

> *...the first tractor biplane for land use built by the Curtiss company and is unquestionably the fastest biplane in the world. Surfaces twenty-four foot wide and four feet deep (chord) speed seventy-five miles per hour. Lincoln Beachey under whose directions the machine was built made the trials.*[10]

But the deaths of imitators continued, and the press began to blame him for almost every aviation fatality. Even his many lovers could not console him. And May was suing her philandering husband for divorce.

Beachey continued to tour to thunderous applause and admiration; not everyone was down on him. Carl Sandburg, as yet an unknown poet, was inspired by Beachey's performance in Chicago. His poem, first published in 1916 reflects the feat and awe with which most men regarded the daring aviator.

To Beachey, 1912

Riding against the east,
Averring, steady shadow
Purrs the motor-call
Of the man-bird
Ready with the death-laughter
In his throat
And in his heart always
The love of the big blue beyond.

Only a man,
A far fleck of shadow on the east
Sitting at ease
With his hands on a wheel
And around him the large gray wings.
Hold him, great soft wings,
Keep and deal kindly, O wings,
With the cool calm shadow at the wheel.

—Carl Sandburg

Notes

1. Hillery Beachey Collection, San Diego Aerospace Museum.
2. Ibid.
3. Ibid.
4. Ibid.
5. Ibid.
6. Martin Cardin, *The Barnstormers*, "A Pack of Jackals," p. 25.
7. Hans Christian Adamson, "The Man Who Owned the Sky" in *True Magazine*, February 1953.
8. Ibid.
9. Ibid.
10. Glenn Curtiss Museum Archives.

BEACHEY FLYING IN THE USA

Postcard photos of Beachey flying as master of the skies.

DAYTON, OHIO FAIRGROUNDS, AUGUST 1914

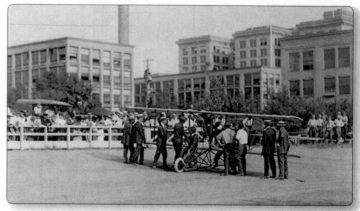

Ready for take off...

...there he goes...

...up into the skies!

Up, up, and away...

...coming in for landing...

...all safe and sound on the ground.

Lincoln Beachey, in a rather funereal portrait made about the time of his divorce, when he was being blamed for the deaths of pilots who tried to imitate his stunts. No wonder he looked gloomy. *Courtesy San Diego Aerospace Museum*

The Pacemaker for Death

Early in 1913, May Beachey was finally granted her divorce. In the court proceedings, she had listed 32 cities in which Lincoln was said to have had affairs before the judge interrupted her and ruled in her favor. And she didn't know the half of it. The local headlines read, "Aviator's Conquest Not of Air Alone."[1] May received a $25,000 settlement and returned to her hometown in Ohio.[2]

The deaths continued and people still called him crazy. Instead of recognizing him as a master artist, they scorned him as the pacemaker for death.

The San Diego Union editorialized:

The San Diego Union

THE PIONEER NEWSPAPER OF SOUTHERN CALIFORNIA

SAN DIEGO, CALIFORNIA, FRIDAY MORNING, JANUARY 3, 1913

TALK OF INJUNCTION AGAINST BEACHEY

Should Lincoln Beachey, the daredevil birdman, be enjoined by the courts from attempting his aerial pursuits? Is Beachey setting an example which will lure scores of

Lincoln Beachey reads an account of his own retirement in *Aero and Hydro,* the leading magazine for aviation. *Courtesy San Diego Aerospace Museum*

his fellow flyers to their death? Should the courts stop him in the name of humanity? Is it their duty to the United States government, many of whose brave aviators may go to their death in attempting to emulate the freak flyer from San Francisco?

Should Beachey be prevented from killing himself? For his own sake, is it the duty of society to restrain him?

City Prosecutor Glidden said a suit might be brought against Beachey for "alienating the affections of rival aviators from their lives."

These are the questions being asked as a result of Beachey's wild performances over the last year. And there is serious doubt as to whether Beachey should be allowed to continue.[3]

Lincoln could not imagine how the public sentiment could be so narrow, nor fathom how he was being so misunderstood. His attention was still fixed skyward. He had a vision of complete freedom in the sky, to turn any way at any time, not limited by power or aircraft fragility. He dreamed of the impossible: to fly upside down, to loop the loop, to fly straight up.

In early May 1913, Lincoln went to Glenn Curtiss in his new San Diego plant to discuss with his boss the possibility of building a machine that would fly upside down and loop the loop. Because both the oil and the gasoline were fed to the motor by gravity, the mechanical problems of fluids management seemed impossible to solve. And Lincoln's reputation as the herald of death cast a pall on Curtiss Aviation as well. Just as Beachey was convincing Curtiss that mob mentality could not impede progress, they were interrupted by the news that another fellow birdman, Charlie Walsh, died nearby, trying "to do a Beachey." Curtiss refused to attempt to build Lincoln's dream.

Lincoln and his promoter Bill Pickens boarded a train to San Francisco. He was scheduled to be the guest of honor at an event at San Francisco's Olympic Club, but he wasn't looking forward to it. Frustrated and confused, he did not notice a grieving young woman with two small children at her side as he changed trains in Los Angeles. She recognized Beachey, however, and her expression changed from grief to hatred as she ran toward him screaming his name.

"Mister Lincoln Beachey, do you know who's on this train you're boarding? Do you have any idea what you've done to my husband? Your friend, your fellow birdman, Charles Walsh, is in this baggage car, in a coffin! Did you know that, Mr. Beachey? You made Charlie do it!" Mrs. Walsh started beating on Lincoln's chest. "You made him do it! You killed my husband!" and she collapsed into the arms of a stranger.[4]

Lincoln collapsed into pure shock and depression. Boarding the train, he rode silently. After about an hour, he took a folded piece of paper from his pocket and started reading to his manager, "God punish you, Lincoln Beachey. Gene would be here with me now if he had never seen you fly." Lincoln explained, "Ely's wife sent me this letter. How can she accuse me, Bill? You know what I thought of Gene. He was like a brother to me."

Pickens tried to protest, but Lincoln silenced him. Taking a piece of paper and a pencil from his coat pocket, he started to write. After a while, he handed the paper to Pickens. "There it is, Bill, the names of 24 men. And I have newspaper clippings that say I killed them all."[5]

The next day Lincoln sent a telegram to his boss:

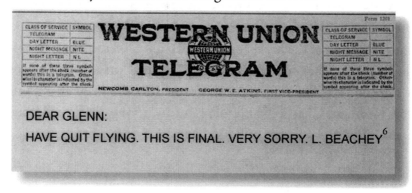

DEAR GLENN:

HAVE QUIT FLYING. THIS IS FINAL. VERY SORRY. L. BEACHEY[6]

May 12, 1913. The Olympic Club in San Francisco was proud to welcome as its guest of honor the greatest birdman of them all. Opening the evening ceremonies, the toastmaster announced, "And now, gentlemen, please join me in welcoming the man who has written aviation history, San Francisco's own, the incomparable Lincoln Beachey!"

Thunderous applause greeted Lincoln as he rose from his seat of honor and walked to the podium, his reticence barely concealing his turbulent feelings. Placing his notes before him, he clenched the speaker's stand, cleared his throat and began to speak.

"Gentlemen . . . I am through with flying!"[7] He was relieved finally to have said it. People in the audience turned to each other in confusion and disbelief. Lincoln raised his hand for silence.

> You could not make me enter an aeroplane at the point of a revolver. I'm done!
>
> There was only one thing that drew crowds to my exhibitions—a morbid desire to see something happen. They all predicted I would be killed and none wanted to miss getting in on it. They bet and the odds were always against my life. They called me Master Birdman but they paid to see me die.
>
> I have just been asked by a syndicate to fly in Europe. I could easily make at least $100,000 on one contract, but I have refused. I will never fly again. Fear has driven me out of the skies for all time. Not fear of my own death or the fear of bodily injury for myself has made me give up an art which I dearly love, but the blame and remorse for the death of brother aviators who went crashing into eternity trying to "out-Beachey Beachey." I have quit as the pacemaker for Death.
>
> I invented the vertical drop, or as the newspapers call it, the Dip of Death, the Dutch Roll, the Ocean Roll, the Turkey Trot, and the Figure Eight, which is also known as the Spiral and Reverse. Death taught me each one of them. Nine of my close friends were spurred on to try these things, and every one of them is dead. Phil Parmalee, John Frisbee, Rutherford Page, Horace Kearney, Billy Badger,

Eugene Ely, Charlie Walsh, Cal Rodgers, and Cromwell Dixon, fine boys all of them. And one by one they have hurtled down, clutching at the robes of God, to smash on earth!

Death has left me alone, has allowed me to do impossible things, because I was a good servant to him. I am tormented with a desire to Loop the Loop in the air. I know that I can do it, but I know that no one else can do it. I know that if I ever go up into the air again I will pull off this Loop the Loop. And then many men will be taken by Death in trying to do the same thing because I have done it.

Death was always my opponent, and I gave tremendous odds. My life was always my own stake—my life against a few dollars. It isn't wisdom that makes me quit. It's deadly fear for others.

In Chicago last September Kearney's mother begged me not to teach Horace any more tricks. Kearney turned and said, "Mother, I must be a top-liner. I must be as good as Beachey or take a back seat. I must try the same tricks he does."

Three months later he was dead.

The wife of Charlie Walsh begged him to cut out the spiral. "Beachey does them," he said. "I too must do them if I am to get the money."

Charles was doing the reverse spiral two weeks later and a wire snapped; they picked him up dead. I felt that I had murdered poor Charlie.

A few days ago I passed through a train station where I saw his widow and two babies. Mrs. Walsh became hysterical. "You made Charlie do it," she yelled at me.

At Tanforan last November I heard several of the boys in the hangars talking about doing the straight glide. I wanted to leave the field then, because when I warned them they only laughed, and I was in the grip of fear—not for myself, but because I was certain they would follow my lead and go to their deaths.

Why then did I enlist as Death's pacemaker? Well, listen. The people demanded thrills in the first place. I was never egotistical enough to think that the crowds came to witness my skill in putting a biplane through all the trick-dog stunts. There was only one thing that drew

Nine Men Killed by Imitating His Desperate Feats. Lincoln Beachey, the World's Most Daring Aviator, Tells Why He Is Afraid to Fly Again

them to my exhibitions—the desire to see "something happen"— meaning, of course, my death. They all predicted that I would be killed while flying, and none near wanted to miss being at the death if they could help it. They paid to see me die. They bet I would, and the odds were always against my life, and I got big money for it.

My Death Dip—the vertical glide—started through an accident that happened to me when I was thousands of feet in the air. I was in Los Angeles, high above the clouds. It was very wonderful, for below, as far as the eyes could see, was a perfect sea of cloudy fleece that reflected the golden sun in a dazzling way. I felt like an angel—so much so that in the ecstasy of the moment I began to sing aloud. And in a twinkling Death seemed to creep upon me and reach out and touch me with a bony finger. My motor had stopped dead!

It is beyond my powers to describe my feeling in that dread moment. Every move for self-preservation flashed before me—I began to drop, drop, drop with ghastly speed. Resolved to die calmly, I tilted the nose of the plane down at an angle and began to glide. Through the clouds I whizzed, the wings of my plane groaning as in very agony from the strain of the resisting air, which rushed through the taut wires of the machine until it sounded as if some great unseen angel of death was playing my requiem on a giant harp.

The memory of it all is now but a mad, dizzy whirl through space. I know I came down out of the heavens with the swish of a great condor. I could hear the hysterical applause as I turned up the nose of my plane to ease the force of my drop from the blue. I had come down in a straight glide at an angle of about 45 degrees. When I stepped down from the machine I didn't dare ask—I just waited for someone to say, "Why, Beachey, old man, your hair has turned snow white!"

And that was the beginning of the Dip of Death. It was the forerunner of all that people pleased to call my air devilry. My defense of the Dip of Death is that I was forced to take it, as birdmen have since. When I kept it up I was furthering the interests of science in that I was showing airmen that it was possible to cheat death when your motor stalled above. It was all at the peril of my own life and at the cost of all the lives snuffed out in my wake. Consequently, I held little fear of an engine gone wrong thereafter, and one-half of the martyrs of this great science would be alive today had they studied the possibilities of the glide as I did, patiently and scientifically.

As soon as I found that I could make the tremendous glides to earth, I began to reinforce my machine. I doubled every wire and gradually I was able to come down at sharper and sharper angles. I went slow. The others didn't.

As the days and weeks and months went by and I was sharpening the angle of that glide, I knew the time would come when I could make a sheer dive from a great altitude.

At first I had great difficulty in breathing. It was hard to control my senses and to get used to the increased air pressure. Gradually I mastered it. One day, letting only a few friends know of my intentions, I determined to make a dead drop from an altitude of 5,000 feet. Well, if I had failed I wouldn't be here to tell about it now. I came straight down like a stone. As I neared the ground I turned up the plane's nose and landed in a distant part of the field as gently as a bird.

And I've done it hundreds of times since. No living thing has ever gone through the air at the rate I went. One day we figured the speed of the drop. From an altitude of 5,000 feet until the time I brought up the plane's nose near the ground I traveled at the rate of 156 miles an hour. Just twenty-three seconds it took to cover the distance!

The boys who tried to follow me in that drop, in most cases, went at it blindly. Before taking up the plane I had been a dirigible balloon operator for five years. Study of the air was not a fad with me. When I took up planes I knew a little more than my brother birdmen. Most of those killed had never been off the ground in anything. Some of them didn't even take the trouble to look their machines over before going up. Generally they left it to a mechanician. I never failed to examine everything before trusting myself to chance.

I watched Rutherford Page trying out some of my stunts in a brand-new Curtiss machine. He was foolishly brave and I tried to warn him. He laughed at me. He insisted that he could do anything I did. As I helped to untangle his dead and broken body from his crashed machine, his mechanician turned to me and said, "Mr. Beachey, Rutherford said just now, before he went up, he was going to out-do your stunts or break his neck."

Just an unexpected puff of wind and it was the end for him. He wouldn't listen, and he paid the price with his life. He was doing what they call my Dutch rolls.

Phil Parmalee was killed doing my Figure Eight. I used to complete the entire evolution with my hands off the levers, guiding my machine with my knees and the motion of my body only. Phil was determined to master that. He died trying it.

Billy Badger, a college student and rich, died in the "pit" in Chicago, during the big Meet. He was all courage and the jolliest fellow I have ever met. He was happy-go-lucky and simply trusted his fate to luck. But he didn't take the trouble to reinforce his wings, and the result was when he tried my vertical drop, the force of the air crumpled his wings about him.

Eugene Ely was showing a Georgia crowd the Dutch roll. When they dug Gene out, his last words were, "I lost control."

Cromwell Dixon, another mere lad, died trying to fly "better than Beachey". He was trying the dip.

John Frisbee went down to his death doing the Ocean Roll.

I was engaged especially to do stunts at the Chicago Meet. My antics made the Meet. There was a betting pool that I would not live out the Meet. When I flew over Niagara Falls and down the gorge they were betting two to one that I would not attempt the feat and five to one that I would never get out of the gorge alive. I did, though, and landed in Canada in six minutes, getting $5,000 for the feat. So perhaps I've been forced to do these stunts.

The aero-scientists said a man couldn't go up in the air and come straight down, because the pressure on the top of the biplane would crush it and turn the thing over. With my hat off to science, I will only say that I dropped straight down daily for two years. Though there was pressure on the top, lots of times I thought the canvas might burst, but it didn't.

The Chief of Police of San Juan, Puerto Rico, whom I know very well in a social way—not through professional attentions—coined the saying: "To fly better than Beachey means death." Those words seemed to be always before my eyes.

I made up my mind that if I did tumble from the air, I did not want my final bump to stamp me as a piker. If it came my time to bow to the scythe wielder, I wanted to drop from thousands of feet. I wanted the grandstands and the grounds to be packed with a huge, cheering mob, and the band must be crashing out the latest rag. And when the ambulance, or worse, hauled me away, I wanted them all to say as they filed out the gates, "Well, Beachey was certainly flying some!"

I love the flying game and believe in it. We can't even dream of the results yet to be attained. I know I've got plenty of courage. I always felt sure of myself—so sure that the thought of death never bothered me. But my conscience won't let me go on with my work. Only one thing will ever tempt me to take my place in an aeroplane. If the United States is forced into a war, and Uncle Sam wants me to fly for Old Glory, I'll fly——but until then I'm through.[8]

The silence of the stunned audience was broken by reporters rushing to call in the news. Beachey's speech was reprinted across the country in hundreds of newspapers. His retirement and the reasons for it echoed around the world.

The extraordinarily exposed and vulnerable position of the pilot out front is clear in this picture from about 1913.

In San Francisco, Lincoln found solace in his daily walks with his mother. They strolled through Golden Gate Park, mother and son, and Lincoln poured his heart out to the one who had loved him before he did anything great.

Lincoln knew he wanted to continue to be involved with aviation, but did not know what form that would take. Soon the answer came. A vaudeville promoter offered him $1000 a week—a year's salary to many—to simply appear on stage with a life size model of his aeroplane, and tell people about aviation, and what he'd been up to for the past year.

Lincoln had not lost his humor, "Tell what I have been up to for the previous year? Why I wouldn't do that for a million dollars a week!"[9]

It was a dream come true for the moment; he got a hefty income and promoted the very thing he felt most deeply about. And it was a dream come true for the promoter. People flocked to hear and see Lincoln Beachey up close. But it was said that among aviators who came, some left with tears in their eyes to have seen the greatest of them all tied to a little stage.[10]

Blanche Scott, the first woman to drive across America, was one of the first women pilots in the country. Lincoln Beachey is on the right.

Courtesy San Diego Aerospace Museum

Notes

1.Hans Christian Adamson, "The Man Who Owned the Sky" in *True Magazine*, February, 1953.

2. Hud Weeks, "An Account of Lincoln Beachey's Life", unpublished.

3. Hillery Beachey Collection, San Diego Aerospace Museum.

4. Adamson, Ibid.

5. Ibid.

6. Glenn Curtis Museum Archives.

7. *San Francisco Chronicle*, May 12, 1913.

8. Ibid.

9. National Air and Space Museum, Smithsonian Institution.

10. Adamson, Ibid.

Lincoln Beachey photos by Frank Carroll. *Author's personal collection*

Beachey with young Frank Carroll
Jr., whose widow provided the
above photos.

Beachey was always
well-dressed for flying.

One of the few pictures of Beachey wearing a felt hat, here worn with
a snappy belted jacket. Fences were always needed to keep the crowds
away from the pilot and his machine. *Courtesy San Diego Aerospace Museum*

Exhibition pilots continued to die attempting feats they weren't prepared for. It was a strange kind of good news as the media no longer blamed Beachey for their demise. Then, in September, four months after his retirement, while playing the

Palace in New York, Lincoln heard news that infuriated him: Pegoud had flown a loop in France! That was to be his glory, and America's claim! Lincoln realized his time off was over. He immediately wired upstate to Glenn Curtiss and told him to start designing a machine that could fly upside down. Curtiss postponed a trip overseas and began work immediately.

Lincoln Beachey,
Master Birdman

Aero and Hydro covered the story of the Master Birdman's decision to fly again.

BEACHEY TO OUTDO PEGOUD

Hammondsport, New York September 1913. Lincoln Beachey will fly again on October 13 at the exercises of the New York Aeronautical Society, commemorating the dicentennial of mechanical flight. Beachey is at Hammondsport, where the Curtiss Aeroplane Co. is building for him the smallest, strongest and fastest biplane so far turned out by the Curtiss Company. Beams and wire cable stays will be twice the usual size, somewhat increasing the weight, but giving the strength demanded for the work Beachey has in mind, which is to outdo, if possible, the recent feats of Adolphe Pegoud. Beachey says that in returning to aviation he had several things in mind; first, the securing of the scalp of the intrepid Frenchman, Pegoud; second, the regaining of his altitude record and other properties that have been trespassed on during this last year; and third, and best, to get into the game he knows best of all.[1]

Even in tiny Hammondsport, people came out in large numbers when Lincoln Beachey was going to fly again, and testing a machine designed to fly upside down and to loop! Concessionaires set up booths, and it seemed that every Sunday picnic lunch in three counties was spread out beside Lake Keuka.

As Lincoln prepared to take off, everyone vied for the best views. Two Navy boys asked Ruth and Dorothy Hildreth, daughters of a wealthy local vintner, to come up on a large tented booth above the crowds for a clear view of the world's greatest airman. They watched

Beachey accidentally hits the
Hildreth sisters sitting atop the tent.

...then crashes his plane.

A kid's box camera captures the tragic moment.

as Lincoln took off directly in front of them and headed out over the
windy lake, framed in early fall colors.

But it was not long before Lincoln headed back. It took him only a
minute to realize his machine was overbuilt, clumsy, and too heavy. As
he approached the field, he banked over the concessions. Suddenly the
plane dropped. His wing clipped the Hildreth sisters, killing one and
critically injuring the other. Immediately, his plane smashed into the

The crowd rushed out to gawk and collect mementos after the crash. Adding to Beachey's anguish. This picture was made into a postcard and sold to thousands of people! *Courtesy Glenn Curtiss Museum*

ground, but miraculously he remained unscathed.[2]

Lincoln's worst nightmare had come true. His flying had actually taken the life of another. Physically and emotionally shaken up, he lay in bed for days. He felt cursed, that death would always plague him. The newspapers scorned him, some of them accusing him of grandstanding and showing off in coming so close to the tents. But most agreed that the accident was simply a terrible tragedy. After four days in bed, Lincoln resolved to make flight as safe as any other form of transportation and rose again.

Curtiss began work on another machine, but winter weather arrived early, forcing them all to move to their San Diego facility. Swarms of newspaper reporters and photographers greeted Lincoln's train at San Diego. "When are you going to do the loop, Mr. Beachey?" "Many scientists think Pegoud uses some kind of optical illusion for his trick." "Orville Wright said that upside-down flying is not possible!" "Some people say you're a fool and only in it for the money."[3]

Lincoln held up his hands to silence them. "When I loop the loop, gentlemen, it will be to demonstrate the unlimited capacity of the fly-

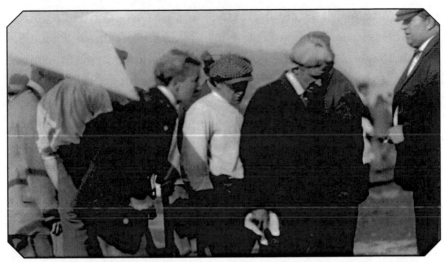

Beachey miraculously walks away from the wreck after he hit the Hildreth sisters during a trial flight in Hammondsport, October 1913. He was only slightly injured, but his face shows deep remorse. *Courtesy Glenn Curtiss Museum*

ing machine. My work is for the sake of the future of aviation and of our country. Like all of my stunts, I will work into the loop gradually. I should be ready for a public exhibition by the Shriner's Jubilee on Thanksgiving Day. I'll be practicing until then with my new plane. That's all I have time for, gentlemen, thank you."[4]

Beachey did as he said. Every day he flew, testing incrementally what the new machine would do and how it felt. Hundreds of spectators and scores of reporters came to witness his daily trials. Then on a breezy November 18th, Lincoln signaled the photographers, "Grease up your cameras boys, and keep your eyes open!"[5]

Beachey climbed to 4000 feet, pointed his machine straight down and dropped half the distance to the ground. Then, instead of pulling up, he pushed forward, making a gradual outside turn, sustaining incredible negative g-forces on his mantle, until his craft was just past horizontal and upside down. The motor fell silent, but Lincoln coasted inverted for nearly a quarter-mile before loss of altitude forced him to flip the plane upright again. Now he knew it could be done. He was on the threshold of a whole new kind of flying. And it had been as simple as he had thought; an illusory barrier to a new frontier. He reported to the press upon landing, "Flying upside-down isn't much. I thought it a bit rough on the collar bones, but upside-down flying is just the first step to looping the loop. I intend to practice for another full week before going for the loop."[6]

Five days later, tragedy struck again. Near the Curtiss camp was the Army Air Corp Field, where the military trained in their antiquated Wright machines. The seasoned Lieutenant E. L. Ellington was instructing his student, Lieutenant Kelley, how to rise more efficiently, when the engine of their plane started to misfire and lose power. When it kicked back in, the sudden turbulence from the propellers tipped up the rear of the machine and pointed the craft downward. The plane fell into a spiral and smashed into the ground. Lincoln and the Curtiss team were the first to reach the crash. As they pulled the bloody bodies from the wreckage, Lincoln pounded his fists on the plane's tattered wing. "Slaughter! Shameless neglect! Our government murdered these men!"

The San Diego Evening Tribune described the tragic accident in exacting detail and published Lincoln's letter condemning the nation's blind disregard of aviation's development.

Aviators Hurled 80 feet to Earth

Two intrepid navigators of the air—Lts. Hugh Kelley and E.L. Ellington attached to the Wright Camp of the First Aero corps, were instantly killed at North Island at 7:33 o'clock yesterday morning, when they fell from an altitude of 80 feet in a Wright dual control biplane. Whether at this instant the unfortunate aviators temporarily lost control of the machine, or the initial impetus of the revolving propeller with the machine at such a slow altitude caused the plane to tip forward, can only be conjectured.

Kelley Buried to Hips

Kelly, in an effort to resist the terrific impact, braced himself as the machine neared the ground. When the wreckage was removed it was found that the aviator had been driven into the soil up to his hips. Both aviators were badly crushed by the engine, which became partly unseated and fell forward, pinning the unfortunate bird-man to the ground. While the impact probably killed the men, the motor made death doubly sure by crushing their chests in a terrible manner.

The mutilated bodies were tenderly removed from the wreckage and carried to the Curtiss camp. The remains were then brought across the bay to the mortuary of Johnson, Connell and Saum.

Biplane is Burned

As is the custom in aeronautics, when an aviator falls to his death, the machine in which Ellington and Kelley fell was burned on the spot where it collided with the earth. The struts, wings, control wires and seats were covered with blood, the wheels cut to ribbons and in fact the whole machine reduced to a mass of kindling wood.

As the bodies of the aviators were being taken across the bay the smoke of the burning machine, which was set afire soon after the two men were removed from the debris, could be plainly seen.

By noon only a pile of ashes marked the spot where the two Army men had given their lives to further aviation.

The machine was burned, it was explained, on account of the depressing effect it would have on aviators if the gruesome debris was hauled back to the hangar and left there for the men to gaze on.

BEACHEY'S DECLARATION:

The parsimonious policy of the United States government in the matter of aviation is responsible for nothing less than the absolute slaughter of good, game men who volunteer to master the science of flying.

The death of Lieutenants Kelley and Ellington yesterday was a result of forcing Army and Navy aviators to fly antiquated machines, or fly nothing at all.

It would be far better if the government would abandon all attempts to school its officers in aviation until such time as congress will appropriate sufficient money to enable the signal corps to properly equip the men with machines and keep such equipment up to the highest point of efficiency. Now they are being sacrificed upon the altar of penury.

I have stood around the aviation camp and noticed the signal corps aviators patching up old machines and trying their level best to make a good flying machine out of scrap material. When I learned, by accident, that the lives of the men were being risked because they could not get proper materials, and that gasoline was scarce at times, I felt ashamed of my government.

Lots of small town post offices and plenty of pork barrel appropriations and but a few paltry dollars for aviation, the hope of future supremacy in warfare. It is unbelievable that such a country boasts great prestige.

I wired the secretaries of war and the Navy in the best of faith. I know that I can teach great lessons in aviation and can demonstrate to members of congress as individuals of the great things of which the aeroplane is capable.

To spend three months in the service would be a great sacrifice to me from a financial viewpoint, but I will gladly do it.

> Japan spends ten times as much each year on aviation as is spent by the United States. Even Mexico has a larger air force. Aviation is either a great agency or it is of no use. If it is of vital importance, why not go into it in the right way, and if of no use why waste any time or money on flying?
>
> The backwardness of our statesmen drove the Wrights to Europe in 1908 to market their inventions. Now it has almost driven Curtiss to the other continent. While he is selling a hundred machines to Italy, Russia and France, he has sold only three to our government recently, and so close was the bargaining that he did not make a cent on the sale.
>
> I demand an inquest into this situation at once. I will come to Washington at my own expense and testify as to what I have seen and to what I think should be done.[7]

The deaths of his fellow aviators increased Lincoln's resolve to take the danger out of flying. Lincoln knew it when he strapped himself into his aeroplane, two days before Thanksgiving. He rose high into the sky, then dived until he had plenty of speed, pulled back on his controls, coming level, then up, back, over, and gently topped his loop. Coming round, Lincoln knew that he could outfly the birds. It was not just a personal moment; it dawned on him that finally humanity could truly fly fearlessly and freely.[9] Mysteriously, he felt he flying dreams of billions had somehow been answered.

This was the moment he had waited for, but it did not end. It was not a moment, but the beginning of a new frontier. His former flying seemed suddenly mild. Instantly he knew he wanted the world's first fully aerobatic flying machine, a motor that would work upside down and unbreakable wings.

On Thanksgiving Day, the Master Aviator astounded San Diego with repetitive loops, and made world-wide news. Lincoln also received a telegram from Washington, responding to his public demand for a

Lincoln Beachey was the first aviator to do repetitive loops, astounding the world.

federal investigation of the deaths of Lts. Kelley and Ellington. Things seemed finally to be going right. On December 2, 1913, Lincoln spoke before Congress, pleading the case for aviation development.

Back in California, Lincoln flew every day, testing the limits of the Curtiss. And as he flew, a new frontier was revealed to the public. The greats do not merely repeat themselves.

L incoln was back in San Francisco for Christmas. Earlier in the year, his mother had restored him to himself, and now she received him proudly. During another of their long walks, her son revealed another maturity: Lincoln wanted another kind of love—a woman, not a girl; a wife, not a girlfriend.

Merced Walton, 1913
Beachey's fiancée

Courtesy of Marie-Merced Thompson, Merced's granddaughter.

As a hometown hero, Lincoln Beachey was a frequent guest of honor at the very highest levels of society. During one of these holiday gatherings, Lincoln met twenty-three-year-old Merced Walton. Many years back, Merced's father had taken pity on a horse being beaten on a slick, steep cobblestone hill. Subsequently he fought for animal rights and founded the Society for the Prevention of Cruelty to Animals. He was a strong and tender soul, as was his daughter. But the young lady was more than kind; she also had a wild streak which loved speed, and was often seen at male-dominated places such as racetracks and circuses.[8] Merced Walton captured Lincoln's heart, but she was wise enough to be wary of him, given his reputation. This was a woman to whom he'd have to prove himself. He had met his match.

Goes From Coffee to Cocktails

LOOPING THE LOOP WITH A CUP OF COFFEE
Lincoln Beachey Drinking Coffee at Upside Down Luncheon, and Former State Senator Frank W. Leavitt Watching Him.

Aviator Is Guest of Honor of the Oakland Commercial Club.

Beachey's upside-down flying created quite stir in the press. His flying mastery earned him increasing respect: they called him "Alexander of the Air", "The Man Who Owns the Sky", "The Divine Flyer", "Master Aviator". Everyone was talking about "upside down!" The *San Francisco Examiner* gave its account of an amusing incident:

San Francisco Examiner
Monarch of the Dailies

BEACHEY DINES TOPSIDE DOWN

The dinner was a scintillating success. The guest of honor was carried into the dining room with his head pendant just above the floor by six muscular guests. The roast duck lay on its back, the vegetables were in the covers with the dishes over them and they began with dessert and finished with soup. Yes, it was a great success.

Was it a crazy dinner? It was not. It was just one of those topsy-turvy meals that Lincoln Beachey has to have occasionally because he flies upside-down so much that he is out of practice eating the ordinary way.

Lincoln Beachey was the guest of honor and the others—they who carried him into the dining room in "peduppermost" position—were brother aviators, including Silas Christofferson, Hillery Beachey, Roy Francis and Frank Bryant. Frank Bryant wore glasses, and they insisted on reversing them and putting them on the back of his head. So to carry out the metaphor, he turned his chair with its back to the table, stood on the seat and did an acrobatic backbend with such success that he was able to upset his soup plate and get some of the soup in his hair.

Lincoln Beachey obliged by standing on his head and eating one grape, but nobody believed that he swallowed it until he resumed a normal position in spite of his protestations.[9]

Notes

1. *Aero and Hydro*, October 1913.
2. Hans Christian Adamson, "The Man Who Owned the Sky" in *True Magazine*, Feb., 1953.
3. Hillery Beachey Collection, San Diego Aerospace Museum.
4. Ibid.
5. Ibid.
6. Ibid.
7. *San Diego Tribune*, November 23, 1913
8. Personal interview with a relative of Merced Walton.
10. *San Francisco Examiner*, December, 1913

Beachey returns to San Francisco to show his hometown
the nerve-tingling loop-the-loop.

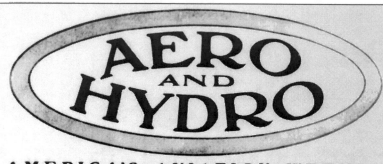

The cover of *Aero and Hydro* magazine, December 1913, showed Lincoln Beachey
at the controls of the first plane to fly upside down. But with the mechanics of
fluid management still in the future, the engine quit when inverted.
Courtesy Hud Weeks Collection

First Fully Aerobatic Flying Machine

S an Francisco was bustling with the preparations for the upcoming 1915 World's Fair, even during the holidays of 1913. The Fair was to open in thirteen months to commemorate the opening of the Panama Canal. The resulting commerce would hopefully provide some relief for a world of growing tensions.[1] President Taft had chosen San Francisco as the site, first signing the bill that authorized the exposition in 1911. The president himself had broken ground for the fair in Golden Gate Park, but shortly thereafter, the site was moved closer to the Bay, atop the marshy land at the bottom of Fillmore Hill. This was to be more than just an international celebration. It was also a triumph for San Francisco, a chance to show the world that the phoenix had indeed risen from the ashes of the 1906 earthquake and fire. Now the city was fresh, beautiful, and more cosmopolitan than ever, the "jewel of the whole world".[2]

The innovations of the turn of the century had a tremendous cultural impact. Automobiles, electric lights, telephones, wireless communication, and moving pictures would all be showcased at the fair, just as the rebuilt San Francisco had incorporated these into the new city. The aeroplane was the epitome of man's achievements, and Exposition officials asked Lincoln if he would be the headline performer every day for the 10-month run of the fair.

Beachey flew past the Pan Pacific International Exposition, under construction in December, 1913.

To be the main attraction at such an occasion was a once-in-a-lifetime opportunity. He gladly accepted their invitation, and agreed to return a year later. Until then, Lincoln would tour America and encourage his crowds to write to their congressmen that the time for a commitment to the future of aviation had come. And then the rest of the world would come to see him at the fair the next year.

Because of the growing problems in Europe, the fair became a symbol of peace: "Peace through Commerce" droned hopefully as if to keep the whole world from falling into the hell of war. The countries of Europe were preparing for war and investing in the development of aviation. But the US government remained at a virtual standstill. Germany, Russia, and France each supported an air force of more than a thousand planes while the US poorly maintained a mere twenty-three.

Architectural designs for the Fair were based on the classical buildings of Europe and the Far East. Planning was extensive, with Henry Ford in charge of machinery, Thomas Edison in charge of electricity and Luther Burbank in charge of horticulture. One of the Fair's premier engineering showcases, The Palace of Machinery, would display a very long promenade of the most advanced mechanical devices in history. The building itself was the largest framed structure on earth. Impressed by its tremendous shell, Lincoln suggested a fabulous challenge for the new year: on New Years Eve, Beachey would attempt the world's first indoor flight. The *San Francisco Examiner* covered with quaint amazement the first flight where weather did not matter.

San Francisco Examiner
Monarch of the Dailies

BEACHEY FLIES INSIDE EXPOSITION BUILDING

Takes New Dare At Death Among Girders

Lincoln Beachey, whose quest for new sky-hazards has led him to the performance of the most amazing aeroplane feats ever achieved, drove his machine through the jaws of death yesterday and is still on his feet.

In the presence of several hundred spectators, who braved a blinding rainstorm, Beachey made aeroplane history by flying within the completely enclosed Palace of Machinery, on the Panama-Pacific Exposition grounds. Almost within a hand's reach of long avenues of great, arching girders, when even a mislaid finger's weight would have meant death, he guided his powerful machine with the calmness of a nursemaid wheeling a perambulator.

There was no wavering or lurching in the swift, clean-cut ascent. For about 100 yards he winged a straight flight at a height of 20 feet.

FEAT WAS A HAZARDOUS ONE

Beachey performed his hair-raising feat under the most adverse circumstances. His little cannonball plane carries a 100 horse-power engine and flies through the air at a speed of seventy miles an hour. Even a layman can see that this is no sort of an affair on which to ride through a maze of arches and girders.

Furthermore, the landing area of the 962-foot arch, where the flight was ended, was slippery with water that had dripped through the roof and his foot brake was rendered useless.

Dropping from the air at a terrific speed, Beachey shot toward the end wall on the skidding wheels. The plane tore through three long strips of cloth, held across his pathway like a tennis net by his mechanicians, with apparently no diminution of speed. The blank wall loomed ahead like a stone buttress.

CROWD LOOKS FOR SMASH

The crowd surged into the archway, waiting for the smash. The plane skimmed along merrily to within a few feet of the wall, when Beachey, by throwing his entire weight against the little foot brake, caused a halt and lurch which brought the car against the wall with comparatively harmless impact. The front wheel was damaged, but otherwise the machine was as sound as ever and Beachey was uninjured.

"I made the flight to demonstrate the absolute control of an aeroplane in the hands of a man who knows how to fly," said Beachey. "Of course, any one can see that a lurch to right or left would mean a smash, as I was flying within a width of 75 feet; but I know I can keep my machine on an absolutely straight course. On a dry floor I could easily have come to a stop before striking the wall."[3]

In his endless quest to do things that had never been done before, Beachey flew inside the Palace of Machinery during the construction for the 1915 World Fair, as a crew of workmen and spectators waved.
Courtesy Hud Weeks Collection

It was a new year, and Lincoln felt as if the whole world lay at his feet. Although acknowledged as the world's greatest aviator, he felt he had just begun. As soon as he had a motor that would stay on upside down, he stated, he would advance the science of aviation by ten years. With a fully aerobatic flying machine, he could eliminate the lag in aviation brought upon by the legal wrangles with the Wrights. Lincoln imagined a company of his own, developing high performance aeroplanes and demonstrating them as the world's best.

In January 1914 the Wrights won what appeared to be a total victory in their patent fight. A United States Court of Appeals judge recognized the Wrights as 'pioneers in the practical art of flying heavier-than-air machine' and ruled that their patent claims covered the use of ailerons as well as wing warping. Curtiss was permanently enjoined from the manufacture or sale of airplanes with ailerons operating simultaneously to produce differing angles. The Wright Company immediately announced its royalty terms: 20 percent on every airplane sold in America. Orville, who disagreed with the company's Wall Street backers on how tight a monopoly to establish, indicated that he would apply a 'policy of leniency' for most manufacturers. But not for Glenn Curtiss.[4]

Henry Ford visiting Glenn Curtiss, and his hydroplane, to help him with his battle with the Wrights.

Aviation enjoyed a new popularity in America, but was still being hampered by the newly-formed Wright Company. Orville retired to Ohio. The new company, now managed by New York businessmen, required all of the country's flyers to obtain a Wright license and pay a royalty before continuing their exhibitions.

In Hammondsport, Curtiss was reeling from his loss to the Wrights. If he consented to pay the exorbitant fees, his manufacturing company would go bankrupt. Curtiss's situation prompted the famous inventor, Henry Ford, to personally come to Hammondsport and offer his help in fighting unfair patents. Ford's patent attorney pointed out that the Wright patent had described their horizontal control (wing warping— literally twisting the wings like a bird's wings) as a *simultaneous* action on both wings. Merely by separating the action of the ailerons, Curtiss was able to appeal the case and continue selling his machines.[5]

Lincoln also protested the judgment on the Wright case. The Wrights had not invented flying; Langley's partial success had proven that. Wanting to set the record straight, Lincoln offered to resurrect and fly Langley's machine, now in a Smithsonian back room. It would prove once and for all that Orville could rightfully claim a patent only on his wing-warping design—not on flight itself or even lateral control. "Give me a barn door and enough power and I'll fly that!"[6] America's premier birdman argued. Glenn Curtiss heard about Beachey's point and in March, 1914, wrote Lincoln. "I am told that you offered at the time of the Wright decision to fly the Langley machine. I believe this would be a good thing to do, and I think I can get permission to rebuild the machine. Of course it did not have a mechanical means of balancing laterally, proving the fact that it is a practical flying machine, which would go a long way toward showing that the Wrights did not invent the flying machine as a whole but only a balancing device, and we would get a better decision next time. Let me know if you are serious in this and if so we will take the matter up with the Smithsonian."[7]

Inspired by Lincoln's suggestion to fly the Langley machine, Glenn made contact with the Smithsonian and began to resurrect the Langley machine in order to help fight the patent case.

Lincoln Beachey and his designer, Warren Eaton, check out Glenn Martin's new plane, a "tractor" type biplane with the motor and propeller in front, and the pilot trapped in the curiously named "cockpit" behind the motor. This was a radical departure for Lincoln , who had always sat out front, facing the wind and weather. His test flight in the new plane was not exactly a triumph. But the motor that spun really impressed him.

Courtesy San Diego Aerospace Museum

Just after his twenty-seventh birthday on March 3rd, Lincoln formed his own company, with Bill Pickens as his promoter, and hired his own crew. Japan offered him $100,000 to come and give them five shows for the royal family and the royal military. And Australia offered him $50,000 for one day of exhibition. A quick tour of the Pacific would be unbelievably lucrative, and he decided he could probably fit it in.

One thing still eluded Beachey: a motor that would perform in any position. He received a telegram from Glenn Martin, an aeroplane designer and builder in Santa Barbara, saying he had such a motor and with it had built Beachey's dream machine. Martin invited Beachey to come and put it through its paces. Lincoln and his own designer/builder, Warren Eaton, immediately went to check it out. It was very promising—a beautiful European type craft with the pilot in the rear and the motor out front: terrible for visibility, but safer. It was very similar to the

Beachey Tractor that he and Curtiss were developing. But the motor was the dream come true, a seven-cylinder French Gnome rotary, with an unusual design. Both the propeller <u>and</u> the engine rotated around a still hollow axle that provided a gasoline/ Castor oil mixture for both fuel and lubrication. Because the entire motor spun there was no up or down for it. But the Castor oil was mixed with the gasoline, and hot oil spewed out of the spinning cylinder on the exhaust cycle. Any Castor oil accidentally consumed gave the pilot an unwanted cleansing of the alimentary canal. The aviator was forced to wear goggles and protective clothing.

Glenn Martin sold 5000 tickets to the trial run of his new machine and invited the press. At first, it flew quite well. Lincoln did ten consecutive loops, breaking his record of seven. But when he flipped the machine on its back and flew upside down, the controls stuck, and Lincoln Beachey could not right the craft. Realizing his pressing predicament, he quickly guided his upside-down craft into the springy branches of an enormous tree. "There was a crash like the collision of a train as the force of the impact uprooted the large tree; everybody thought the end had come to Lincoln Beachey; some stood as if transfixed, hundreds swooned, others cried hysterically, but the morbid ones made a rush through half a mile of marshy ground and they found

New Loop-the-Loop Machine

SPECIAL MARTIN BIPLANE BUILT FOR LINCOLN BEACHEY

Beachey tests Glenn Marin's dream machine, built in Santa Barbara, with a seven-cylinder rotary Gnome motor in front of the pilot, European style.

Courtesy San Diego Aerospace Museum

the world's nerviest man-bird not only alive, but practically unscratched."[8]

Lincoln, however, was very excited about the performance of the Gnome rotary, if understandably disappointed with the aircraft. The gyroscopic effect of engine and prop spinning made the pitch forces immense, but having a motor that provided power when inverted, even for a few precious seconds, won out. Lincoln was so impressed with the motor that he canceled his Pacific trip (and the $150,000) and made immediate plans to travel to the French-German border to acquire the spinning dynamo.

Lincoln Beachey boards the *Lusitania* to sail for Europe in March 1914, to personally purchase two revolutionary Gnome motors for his own new planes. He would be met in France by Gustave Eiffel, who accompanied him to the dangerous German-border factory.

He instructed Warren Eaton to design and build him an aeroplane of the Curtiss Pusher type that could hold the Gnome and stressed to perform in every position. He instructed his promoter Bill Pickens to book him from mid-May to the New Year, anywhere and everywhere. They agreed to meet back in Lincoln's favorite road town, Chicago.

Lincoln traveled across America and boarded the newly-christened British luxury liner, the *Lusitania*. In France, the president of the Aero Club and famous architect, Gustav Eiffel, traveled with him to the Gnome motor factory near the uneasy Germany border and assisted in purchasing two of his country's finest motors.

Lusitania

When Beachey arrived back in New York, the US Aero Club was holding a meeting in Manhattan and urged him to attend.

Airman, Back From Europe, Says He Will Cause City To Gasp Plans Under Way To Form Air Congress

Lincoln Beachey will loop-the-loop in an aeroplane here within thirty days. Not only that, but he promises to give a series of thrill exhibitions such as have never been seen in this country. Beachey arrived from Europe on the Lusitania yesterday and outlined his plans at the McAlpin Hotel last night.

Beachey brought back from France a new 80-horse power Gnome motor of the Monosoupe [single valve] type. He says it is the most efficient motor he can find for his purpose and that he does not wish to be handicapped by the upright type of motor.

"I shall do some exhibition work that will open the eyes of the people as to the possibilities of the aeroplane," said Beachey.

Beachey leaves for Chicago with his manager, "Bill" Pickens, to-day, and will fly on the lake front in about two weeks, prior to coming to New York.

The first steps toward the organization of the International Aeronautical Congress, to be held at the Panama-Pacific Exposition in August, 1915, were taken at a meeting held in the McAlpin last night. The congress is not to be controlled by any club or faction, according to Arnold Kruckman, manager of the Bureau of Aeronautics for the exposition, but will be a general discussion of aviation problems by recognized authorities from all countries. Ten thousand dollars will be devoted to field experiments.

Those present included A. B. Lambert, Hudson Maxim, Captain Thomas S. Baldwin, Alfred W. Lawson, editor of "Aircraft"; Dr. William J. Hammer, Inglas Uppercut, and Lincoln Beachey.[9]

Glenn Marin, left, Lincoln Beachey, second from right, and two member of the design team, pose for a smiling pretest-flight photo, March 1914.

Lincoln took the motors to his crew in Chicago. They installed one in his beautiful, new biplane and the "Little Looper" was born, the first fully aerobatic flying machine. Complete with 5'6" 145 lb. Beachey and 40 minutes of fuel and lubricating castor oil, the Little Looper weighed 773 pounds. The 80 hp Gnome *monosoupape* engine had its

"Little Looper" reconstruction model

Lincoln enjoyed flying the "Little Looper" within inches of any photographer who dared to get on the track.

exhaust valve at the top of each cylinder. Intake was through a port at the base of the cylinder. Engine weight was 205 pounds, and the lubricant was pure Castor oil mixed with the gasoline. The Little Looper had a climb rate of 1,125 fpm and a top (level) speed of 85 mph. The prop was an enormous Flottorp with a diameter of seven feet, nine inches, turning at 1,260 rpm. The engine speed was altered by a foot control that advanced or retarded the timing. The Little Looper wingspan was a scant 21 feet with a constant chord of three feet six inches. The landing gear was of a rigid design and of the tricycle type. The controls were standard Curtiss (albeit beefed up for aerobatic stresses), a shoulder yoke for aileron control, center wheel for elevator and rudder. [10]

Chicago was abuzz with excitement, and masses of people appeared to witness first hand a new aerial dimension. "I am not a reckless aviator," said Beachey to a reporter on May 12, 1914, as he made an air test and announced that he was ready to start. "I don't take a single chance when I am up in the air. That's why I am still here, while the other good boys are gone.

"I never do any experimenting and I never do anything foolhardy—that is, foolhardy from the standpoint of an aviator. Some of the things like looping the loop seem dangerous, but as a matter of fact they are not more so than straight flying.

"I will try to show Chicago just what can be done in a biplane. Those who expect to see an accident will be disappointed. At least I hope so. But I will give them all the thrills they are looking for." [11]

Beachey zooms the Little Looper in front of a crowded grandstand during his glorious tour of 1914. *Courtesy Hud Weeks Collection*

Indeed, 150,000 Chicagoans were stunned by Lincoln's performance. He looped, he spun, he danced and twirled; he shot across the sky like a shooting star.

Lincoln Beachey even flew in ways that still, to this day, have never been repeated. His title as the World's Greatest Aviator remains. The *Sunday Record Herald* recorded the unbelievable feat of the Master Birdman.

SUNDAY MAGAZINE
of the SUNDAY RECORD-HERALD

150,000 Watch Beachey Over Lake

Lincoln Beachey presented a new stunt—the "tail slide"—yesterday while hundreds of thousands in Grant Park cheered.

Beachey's aim is to keep a few steps in the lead of M. Pegoud, the French aviator who "invented the loop the loop."

Beachey had just landed in Grant Park when someone in the crowd remarked "You flew every which way but backwards."

"All right, I'll fly backward for you this afternoon," the pioneer American "upside-down" flier announced.

Stalls Craft In Air

So in the second flight he "stalled" the aeroplane in the air, "sat it down" on its tail, and flew or slid backward for several hundred feet.

Then the broad, stubby tail turned up a trifle. The aircraft stopped dead still in the air and began going forward again, and began falling like a plummet toward the earth.

"Oh! he's falling! He'll be killed!" shrieked several women. A puff of smoke and a roar indicated the restarting of the motor, however, and the little twenty-four-foot machine darted away and continued its aerial romp.

Most Daring Feat

The "tail slide," considered by members of the Aero Club of Illinois as the most daring piece of aerial navigation ever performed, is by far more sensational than the loop. It is a letter "Z" cut in the air, Beachey making the diagonal line with his machine tail first, shooting nearly 100 miles an hour in reverse.

The upper and lower bars are made in a half circle, the biplane being at the apex of a loop when it starts on the long and dangerous drop.

Not even members of the Aero Club, under whose auspices Beachey is making his flights, knew that he was to try a new feat. Even they, when the noise of the motor ceased, feared he had lost control of his craft.

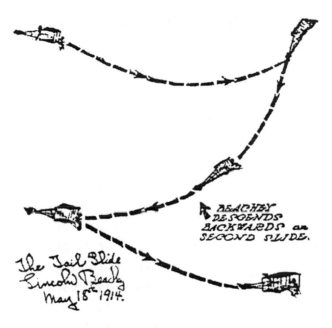

This diagram, printed in several newspapers in 1914, was an artist's attempt to illustrate the impossible: flying backwards! No one had done the tail slide before, and no one has ever done it like this since.

Courtesy San Diego Aerospace Museum

Plans More For Today

Unconcerned, the daring aviator took his seat, resolved to "give the crowd a run for its money," as he afterward put it.

He had been planning the "tail slide for a long time." Even while he was supervising the work on the machine he was planning sensational features. To-day, the last of his Chicago engagement, he will attempt two more thrillers, but would discuss neither of them last night.

Ninety-degree banks, the tango and upside-down spiral dives made up the balance of yesterday's program, but all were pushed into the background by the new slide.[12]

Another newspaper gave a slightly more belligerent slant to the story, and quoted Beachey at length.

INTREPID AIRMAN DECLARES THAT SCIENTISTS DON'T KNOW EVERYTHING

Lincoln Beachey's pet hobby is upsetting the theories of scientists and laughing in the faces of the wise men who figure out aviation's limitations from rocking chairs.

Beachey flying upside down at Grant Park

The Wrights and Curtiss declared positively that it was a scientific impossibility to loop the loop, fly upside-down or make a vertical drop in an aeroplane—without the pilot being picked up beneath his machine. Learned men met Beachey's claim that he had dived 5000 feet from the sky in a vertical drop, with the declaration that man could not live to reach the bottom of such a drop. It was even pointed out that a man falling from the top of a ten-story building would die before he hit the pavement. But Beachey did all these things with the exception of trying to disprove the ten-story building theory, and then added something brand new.

Here is what the fearless birdman had to say.

"I have done something new. I call it the "tail slide." When I started up on my last trip I wasn't quite decided as to what I would do. I pulled back on the control while I was going up and I soon had my machine standing per-

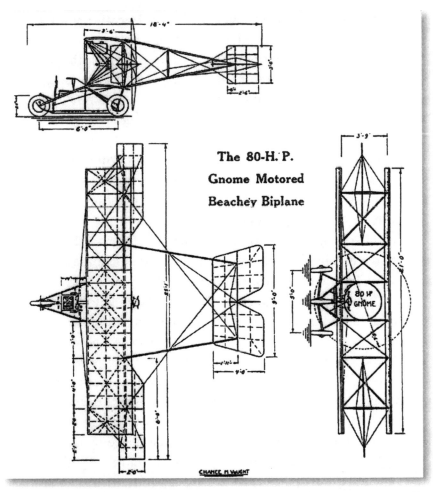

The design for the Gnome biplane kept the pilot out front and the propeller to the rear, the standard Curtiss design. From *Aero and Hydro*, May 23, 1914.

pendicular. I was then about 2,500 feet in the air.

"Then I decided what I wanted to do. I even decided on the name for the stunt, the "Z". I let go and slid back on the tail, all the time pulling still further back on the control, because I was going in an opposite direction.

"It was one of the most graceful drops I have ever made. There was my aeroplane standing exactly perpendicular and dropping down and down. When I got almost to the ground I shot the control forward again and at a terrific rate sped forward and gradually downward.

"Several asked me after it was all over whether the tail slide was as dangerous or more so than looping the loop. I think it is about the same, because in my opinion neither one is dangerous except in windy weather and when a man loses his head at the wheel.

"I want to show such men as Henry Ford, Thomas Edison and other inventive and manufacturing geniuses how I handle the Little Looper. I do not believe they dream such things are possible. Instead of being a reckless chance-taker, I am really the pioneer explorer of the unchartered air lanes of the sky. My tour this summer will help advance the science of flying by ten years.

"I wish I could get a few of those scientific fellows aloft in my machine. They try to make me out to be a foolish adventurer of the sky when they do not even know what they are talking about. Theory is one thing and practice is another. The fastest speed credited to a human in a mechanical vehicle is chalked up to Burnham, the automobilist. He is supposed to have covered a mile at the rate of 142 miles an hour. He performed the feat only once.

"I have made more than 100 drops from the sky at the rate of 180-210 miles an hour. My machine weighs about 800 pounds and when it is in a vertical position there is but a slight surface resistance. Imagine such a load dropping from a mile high, straight down. The speed is far greater than anyone can possibly imagine, for no human save myself has ever traveled that fast. I have no protection from the wind and until I schooled myself through long practice to take two short breaths during the trip, I was unable to breathe at all.

"It requires just 18 seconds to made the drop and so terrific is the pressure on my chest that I am compelled to wear a fiber protector to prevent the breath from being knocked out of me. It required three months' time for me to master this drop. I sent the biplane down at a slightly steeper angle each time until at last I was dropping straight down. There were those who would not believe me when I told them I was doing the drop. A year ago it was the piéce de résistance of my repertoire. Now the loop the loop and upside-down flying overshadow the 'death drop' to such an extent that I do not brag about it anymore. But just the same it is the hardest thing I do, and the one trick I fear more than the rest. But that same dive was the thing that demonstrated it was possible to perform the loop and to fly upside-down. I shall never call it a back number for I learned too much about the aviation game while performing it."[13]

When the Wright brothers won their court battle, they also required every flyer to get a permit from them. Lincoln wanted to avoid any possible obstruction to his exhibition flying, and complying with the court's ruling, he applied for the required certification immediately. The Wrights granted a showcase permission to America's premier birdman right away. While in Massachusetts, the *Brighton Herald* carried the story of the only legal pilot in America.

BEACHEY FLIES WITH A WRIGHT LICENSE ONLY AVIATOR SO FAR TO SUCCEED IN GETTING THE COVETED DOCUMENT

Lincoln Beachey did his air feats at Brighton Beach yesterday in the face of a puffy forty-mile gale with the moral support of a flying license from The Wright Company, which controls the aeroplane patents granted to Orville and Wilbur Wright.

Beachey now enjoys the distinction of being the only

aviator flying under a Wright license. His is the first license since the recent patent litigation ended with a declaration in the Wright's favor. The terms of the agreement are $1000 for a license plate for Beachey's machine and $25 dollars for each exhibition day. The agreement holds until the end of this year. As a result, there has been little flying because aviators have been afraid of an injunction from The Wright Company.

T.R. MacMechen, who was at Brighton Beach to see Beachey fly yesterday has just returned from Dayton where he applied to Mr. Wright for a license for the French aviator Pegoud. Pegoud was putting together a series of exhibition flights in this country. Mr Wright did not mince words regarding his attitude toward foreign flyers, according to Mr. MacMechen, and toward Pegoud in particular. He will make it as hard as possible for Pegoud to fly in the country, he told Mr. MacMechen. This is to protect American flyers, Mr. Wright said.[14]

To counter the Wrights' claim on the invention of flight, Curtiss completed the resurrection of the Langley machine and offered Lincoln the honor of flying it off Lake Keuka. Lincoln deferred to Curtiss, who on May 28, 1914, flew the reconstructed (and improved) Langley machine with much fanfare. The adjustments made to the machine for stability were not mentioned. The Smithsonian proclaimed, "The Aerodrome has demonstrated that, with the original structure and power, it is capable of flying with a pilot and several hundred pounds of useful load. It is the first aeroplane in the history of the world of which this can be truthfully be said."[15]

Beachey gives a sour look at a photographer at the Chicago meet. He grew tired of being pestered, yet he always kept brochures handy in his pocket to hand out to fans. *Courtesy Hud Weeks Collection*

Notes

1. Promotional brochures for the Panama Pacific International Exhibition, 1915.
2. Promotional brochures for the Panama Pacific International Exhibition, 1915.
3. *San Francisco Examiner*, December 31, 1913.
4. Curtis Prendergast, *The First Aviators*.
5. Ibid.
6. Martin Cardin, *The Barnstormers*, "A Pack of Jackals" p. 29
7. Glenn Curtiss Museum Archives.
8. Hillery Beachey Collection, San Diego Aerospace Museum.
9. Ibid.
10. *Sport Aviation Magazine*, October 1989
11. Chicago newspapers, Hillery Beachey Collection.
12. *Chicago Record Herald*, May 18th, 1914
13. Chicago newspapers, Hillery Beachey Collection.
14. Ibid.
15. Prendergast, Ibid.

Beachey and Curtiss incorporated the ailerons into the wing surface, instead of positioning them between the wings, in order to avoid legal issues with the Wright Company. *Courtesy Hud Weeks Collection*

The Genius of Aviation

F or the rest of the year, Lincoln flew daily before millions of Americans. Every day he made front-page headlines, towns virtually closed down, railways rescheduled to follow his 126-city tour. With far more than promotional enthusiasm, he distributed tens of thousands of programs at his shows telling of his experiences, and explaining the extreme need for the government to get moving on aviation.

THE GENIUS OF AVIATION

by Lincoln Beachey

I have demonstrated the possibilities of aviation more than three thousand times. I was unable, however, to solve the genius of aviation until I "looped the loop," which feat I accomplished with my aeroplane, for the first time, November 24th, 1913, over San Diego Bay, California, flying from the ground of the government aviation school on North Island, where is stationed the First Aero Corps, attached to the Signal Service.

The Silent Reaper of Souls and I shook hands that day.

Thousands of times we have engaged in a race among the clouds—plunging headlong in breathless flight—diving and circling with awful speed through ethereal space. And, many times, when the dazzling sunlight has blinded my eyes and sudden darkness has numbed all my senses, I have imagined him close at my heels. On such occasion I have defied him, but in so doing have experienced fright which I cannot explain. But now, the old fellow and I are pals.

The instant we had completed the "loop" together I decided that I would fear him no more. It was then that man's courage, coupled with an invention of science, had finally solved the deep mystery which through the ages had surrounded the flight of birds.

Courage at the helm of an aeroplane driven upwards into a loop by the force of propeller blades attached to powerful motors will master the gravity of space. The value of such knowledge to society now rests with men who possess money and brains. I am convinced the aeroplane is a safe and practical vehicle of transportation.

Dirigible balloons and other types of airships, so-called, will have their limitations, while the aeroplane, for the reason of its simplicity in construction and operation will be known as the "flyabout," and like the "runabout" or motordome will become a popular means of conveyance with the masses.

The aeroplane, also, is bound to prove of inestimable value as an agency in warfare, doing scout duty in signal service, and as a weapon of destruction in a variety of forms, for several reasons, one of which is its capability in the attainment and maintenance of tremendous speed.

On the day following my accomplishment of the "loop maneuver" I was honored by the receipt in San Diego of an invitation from Secretary of War Garrison requesting my presence December 2nd, at his office in Washington, D.C. where I reported in due time. In the presence of members of the General Staff I was privileged to have the opportunity of minutely describing certain data I had secured as a result of my perilous flight, pertaining to the science of navigation, the construction of my new type of aeroplane, and its operation.

The Army and Navy departments have engaged in an exhaustive and comprehensive study of the science of aviation. The men at the head and front are thoroughly acquainted with its possibilities, but powerless, absolutely, to develop the science to a state of perfection without sufficient money to do so.

The parsimonious policy pursued by our government in the matter of aviation is directly responsible for its lack of advancement. Its progress is bound to be slow until such a time as members of Congress, a majority, awaken to its infinite value as an agency in warfare and in the affairs of commerce.

The eyes of the nation are focused on the daily press for enlightenment on the question. It is small wonder that hopes are blasted when the harrowing disasters encountered by our Army and Navy men are so ruthlessly depicted in screaming headlines, that we stand appalled at the brink of graves, bewildered and frightened at the mere word—aviation.

It would be far better for our government to abandon all attempts to school its officers in aviation until such a time as Congress will appropriate sufficient money to enable the Signal Corps to properly equip the men with machines and keep such equipment up to the highest point of efficiency. Now they are being sacrificed on the altar of penury.

On numerous occasions I have stood around aviation camps and noticed the Signal Corps aviators patching up old machines and trying their level best to make a good flying machine out of scrap material, and that even gasoline was scarce at times, I felt ashamed of my own government. Our Army boys seem to be forced to take what is handed them, and instead of new machines of the latest and strongest equipment and construction, there are only about three good machines in the lot that comprises the equipment located on North Island, San Diego Bay, California.

Congress last year appropriated $150,000 toward the equipment and maintenance of aviation schools in the signal service. The requisition submitted by the Army and Navy departments called for an appropriation of $1,000,000.

Japan, Italy, Germany and France spend ten times as much each year on aviation as is spent by the United States.

Aviation is either a great agency in war or it is of no use. If it is of vital importance, why not go into it in the right way, and if it is of no use why waste any time or money in flying? And what of the lives of brave men?

I am convinced it is possible to demonstrate to members of Congress as individuals the great things of which the aeroplane is capable. If it were possible to corral 'em—every mother's son—on one of the aviation fields near Washington to witness an exhibition or two of the "loop maneuver," "upside-down flying," "dropping from the clouds" and a few other perfectly simple stunts, I am sure they would have an entirely different opinion of the flying machine. The advancement in aviation then would go forward in leaps and bounds.

Previous to my accomplishment of the "loop maneuver" over San Diego Bay, California, November 24th, Pegoud, a Frenchman, won distinction in his own country by the same maneuver.

But we Yankees, you know, have a habit of going 'em all one better. Parley-vue-what? Since November 24th I have "looped" 268 times.

"Fools! fools!" rings out in clarion tones the voice of the multitude. Ah! — but are we?

"No!" and again "No!" I shout back in defiant answer.

With the knowledge we now possess, there remains no danger. We have loved the mystery which has surrounded the flight of birds, have mastered the gravity of space, have acquired the genius of aviation. It requires only practice, patience and courage to master an aeroplane. And be careful—that's all.

It requires skill, perhaps, to become expert as a bird-man and to acquire the proper knowledge of air currents, equilibrium, measurement of distance and space, engine and steering control, power requirements, as pertains to both engine and rudder as well as the wings of the aeroplane; of resistance force of the machine, as a whole, while flying under full power ahead, upwards or downwards and while driving with a straight drop or dive with power on or off. All this knowledge is necessary, with more, I assure you—as complicated and difficult as it may appear, I may say the aeroplane, insofar as its construction and operation are concerned, presents itself to a novice in form more simple than does the automobile.

And having once acquired the science of aviation through diligent practice and training, physical and mental, the knack of it "stays with you" the same as the art of swimming and the playing of golf and tennis and baseball.

Come along, come along, come with me aboard an aeroplane.

We will fly to a region where men who have courage will find an abundance of peace and good-will. We will fly through the clouds with their lining of gold and pure

In the summer of 1914 in Denver, on a windy day, Beachey needed a large crew to turn his plane into the wind for take-off. *Courtesy Hud Weeks Collection*

silver. We will fly to the skies where the birds through the ages have been welcomed and kissed by the glorious sunlight and where the moonbeams have caressed them and the cool winds and dew have rested and blessed them. It is there in the sky where men of all nations will some day learn the true meaning of brotherly love.

It seems not long ago that I stood on the crest of a mountain and gazed for miles over a magnificent stretch of valley land in Southern California. I was a mere lad then. Across the valley directly opposite me and on a level with my elevation was located the peak of another mountain range. Down in the valley a peace and quiet rest that was beyond my understanding. And, oh! how I longed for the wings of a bird that I could go swiftly and gently deep into that valley and across to the opposite mountain peak.

And just at that moment there burst from the clouds a huge ball of fire atop the horizon. Surely there was gold to be found in abundance where the sun set over the sea, As I stood there in contemplation, enraptured, my gaze wandered far down the valley to the ocean and to an entrancing group of tropical islands some twenty miles from shore. And I wanted to fly there too. And so I decided that some day I would build me a flying machine.

Well, I have done so. I have flown across valleys and over mountains and high up through the clouds full of wondrous gold, and I have experienced quiet and peace—peace that is glorious.

Will you not journey with me?

"I will not!" is the reply I fancy I hear.

Oh, very well. I will call you a coward—just that—and forget and forgive you. And I will dare to say you have not nor will experience life to its fullest until you have taken a trip to the clouds and the skies.

As a matter of fact I know you are simply itching to go. I know this for the reason that in all my experience as a birdman, with all my tricks and daring performances, thousands of times thousands of people have urged me and begged me to take them along. Many times I have done so, on straightaway flights. They have been thrilled with the pleasure, as I, and enchanted. And have wanted some more.

Danger, no doubt, attends every flight of an aviator. Its possibility, however, in straightaway flying is remote and seldom encountered, providing the weather conditions are adaptable and the aviator is careful and sober-minded and that the aeroplane so far as equipment is concerned is in perfect adjustment. Moreover, the type and construction of the flying machine must be considered above everything else.

> **BEACHEY IS THE WONDER OF WONDERS**
> THE GENIUS OF AVIATION
> See Beachey in his wonderful "loop the loop' maneuvers,
> upside down flying, "dropping from the clouds," and
> other daring and startling midair stunts.
> **EVERY ACT IS A THRILLER**
> See Beachey—The Nerve-Tingling, Spine-Chilling,
> Death-Daring, Sensational Beachey
> THREE FLIGHTS ◇ RAIN OR SHINE
> SEE IT ALL FROM THE GRANDSTAND

An advertisement for the Texas State Fair, October 25, 1914.
Courtesy San Diego Aerospace Museum

These factors entirely provide for success and for safety. They alone represent cause and effect—profit and loss. They are responsible, as are members of Congress, for lack of advancement in aviation.

Again, I may say, I am convinced there exists no danger in flying an aeroplane of a type such as I now use. It possesses strength that is rugged and power in its engine and controls that, to my mind, puts the "kibosh" to all danger. In its construction is embodied every element of scientific and mechanical ingenuity that is required in a flying machine. It is possible, no doubt, that improvements in its construction will in time be accomplished, the same as applies to the construction of the automobile, which vehicle of transportation during a ten-year period evolution has advanced with bewildering strides. And it will continue its advancement into a broader state of perfection if it is possible for engineering science to make it so.

The genius of aviation is acquired gradually, and it should be. In fact there can be no other safe rule. In the figurative sense the wings of a novice should be clipped.

He should be satisfied hopping around for awhile. Then let him work along the same lines that govern an apprentice of any sort. Aviators are not born like poets.

A novice at the game of aviation and a cub in the game of baseball are one and the same breed. Both require health of body and mind. Without it, he can not become expert at the game. Such form can be acquired only through a regular course of training and practice. His moral and physical habits must be free of all intemperance and abuse. The eyes of the aviator must be quick and clear, ditto his brain, and his nerves strong and steady.

With just this sort of determination in mind it is possible for anyone, in time, to accomplish any and all of the so-called "fool-hardy flights that I have accomplished. I am not taking the chance or running the risk you imagine. I am an expert in the game of aviation. It would be fool-hardly surely, for a novice to undertake such a flight as "the loop." I possess all the physical and mental requirements. I possess the necessary knowledge acquired through experience and study to make the accomplishments of the feat possible. I know my machines have become familiar with air currents. That I had become thoroughly acquainted with the air, and with the gravity of space, I was not sure until I "looped the loop."

Scientists, through the ages, have claimed and proclaimed that to solve the mystery of gravity was beyond the genius of man and always would be. I have disproven the theory. The truth of the matter is the scientists were not sure—they did not know. They claimed also that the world was round and the existence of the poles of the earth. Such theory was not fact, however, until Columbus and Peary and Scott proved it so.

It is true the science of aviation presents itself even now as a problem that has not been thoroughly solved. We have the winds to consider—to master and harness. To-day, however, we are able to navigate the flying machine through winds the velocity of which, in the early stages of the game, made progress impossible. And some day we will be able to mount and ride any steed of the air, be he ever so tempestuous, for sayeth the prophet Isaiah, "And it will come to pass that to the persevering will come all things from the rising of the sun until the setting thereof." Or words to such effect, I am short of his dope.

Aviation will progress rapidly in these United States of America the instant members of Congress wake up. There exists today, unfortunately, a desire on the part of would-be aviators to witness the appearance of a bundle of assurance, neatly tied with a bundle of blue baby ribbon, the same to be presented them personally and privately from the hands of the Secretary of War, who must be armed to the teeth with rapid-fire weapons, before they will accept aviation seriously.

Now is the time, if you are interested in the smallest degree, to sit down and write a letter to the congressman who represents you in Washington, D.C., urging him to engage himself in the study of the question of aviation. Its advancement will be rapid, providing a proper number of aviation schools are established with proper equipment and instruction in the game is given by experienced and expert aviators.[1]

The "adulation Lindberg was to receive thirteen years later became the day-to-day reality" for America's most thrilling hero, Colonel H.C. Adamson wrote.[2] Triumphant entrances into cities, entertainment at the highest levels of society, and praise to the extreme replaced the scorn and tragedy he had only recently endured. Lincoln continued to write the Secretaries of War and other government officials, asking permission to come to Washington so that he could show them the full possibilities of the aeroplane. He was determined to change the situation.

Meanwhile, Orville Wright publicly declared Lincoln's advertised feats were impossible, probably illusions created high in the sky, a hype to draw the crowds. Lincoln looked forward to Dayton. But an even more famous person would believe what he saw when Lincoln got one of his wishes: the chance to fly for Thomas Edison.

Thomas Edison, circa 1914

BEACHEY'S STUNTS AMAZE EDISON

Thomas A. Edison declares that Beachey's loop-the-loop and upside-down flights are the greatest contributions to science since the Wright brothers first flew a heavier than air machine some ten years ago.

"I was startled and amazed," said Edison, "when I saw that youngster take to the sky and send his aeroplane though the loop and then follow that feat with an upside-down flight. I could not believe my own eyes and my nerves were a tingle for many minutes.

"Two years ago Orville Wright told me that man had done about all with the air-craft that could be done until the inventive genius provided some automatic balancing device calculated to act more quickly than man can think and act at the same time.

"Contrary to my impression, Beachey's loop was not performed high in the air, at a distance that would enhance the opportunity for a trick of legerdemain. But almost over my head he spun around, outraging all wonderful, so wonderful, in fact, that I was relieved when, after the third loop, Beachey came back to the earth.

"Then I spent a whole day figuring out how it was possible for a young aviator to be performing a feat the man who invented and flew the first aeroplane declared was impossible; there was sufficient food for thought, and deep thought at that. When I sought out young Beachey and asked him for an explanation, he looked at me in a quizzical manner and replied, 'I took you for my example and set out to do what others thought impossible. Then after studying it all out, I went at it and combined thought and action to a degree sufficient to get away with it.'

"That tells the whole story, doing what the other fellow declares impossible. And it is a rare sport doing it, too."[3]

Much of Lincoln's tour was in the company of the country's number-one race car driver, Barney Oldfield. They booked themselves in any racetrack they chose, and crowds overflowed the grandstands, and surrounded the event. Beachey began the shows with "ordinary flying"—spirals, dances, swoops, and rolls. It was trumpeted as, "The Championship of the Universe": the race of  sky and earth machines. Beachey would fly within inches of the speeding car and driver, even knocking off Oldfield's hat with his front wheel. Oldfield once commented that he liked racing aeroplanes because they did not kick up dust in his face as did other race cars. Lincoln overheard Oldfield's comments and during his next race banked the turns so steeply and so low that he kicked up racecourse dust with his wing tip, drawing a line in the dust.

How did he fearlessly and flawlessly execute such feats? It was said, "Those aren't his wingtips, those are his fingertips."[4]

SPEED DEMONS TO DEFY DEATH

Barney Oldfield and Lincoln Beachey Staging Thrilling Race for Supremacy at Hamline

There is nothing that can happen high in the air that I cannot get out of with safety if I have enough space to use in dropping while getting the machine under control. But when I am going at a speed of 100 miles per hour just a few feet above the ground, the slightest accident to any part of the machine, or the stopping of the motor for even an instant would send me crashing to the ground at frightful speed before I could even think of what was happening.

That is why I am the only man that puts up such a race with speed wagons and motorcycles. Of course there are others who race autos and aeroplanes, but they sail high and such a contest is about as exciting as a game of beanbag at a church social.

The public expects and demands just a hundred times as much action and chance-taking from me that it does from others. That is the bad feature of having the reputation of being the world's champion dare-devil.

I often touch the driver's head with my front wheel as I pass over him and on the turns I have to bank at an angle of absolute perpendicularity to get around the short turns ahead of the auto.

But to keep ahead of the procession in my game, a fellow must go pretty close to the limit, and I do not intend to let the margin of safety and disaster be any wider than I can help. Beachey never cheats the crowds, that is, excepting those who come to see me die.[5]

BEACHEY VS. OLDFIELD

Lincoln Beachey races Barney Oldfield at the Iowa State Fair in 1914.

Courtesy Hud Weeks Collection

Beachey congratulates Oldfield for a race well lost.

Artists' depictions of the great race between early aeroplanes and automobiles.

Beachey sometimes knocked Oldfield's hat off with his front wheel while zooming past the grandstand at 70 m.p.h. *Courtesy Hud Weeks Collection*

AVIATOR VS. AUTOMOBILIST

Lose your hat again, Barney?

...THEY CAME FROM MILES & MILES TO SEE THE SHOW!

Everyone was enjoying the races!
Seeing things they had never seen before!

Postcards documenting the fun so people could share what they saw.

Beachey used no-hands flying to show the ordinariness of flying,
yet it often frightened his audiences out of their wits.

Orville Wright was coming to Lincoln's show in Dayton, and had been quoted as disregarding the reports of Beachey's supposed feats. But in Dayton, Lincoln's perfection was acute. He ended the show with ten consecutive loops, then flipping his machine on its back, flew it upwards until it stalled, fell, *flew backwards upside down*, stalled backwards upside down, and repeated this stunt —an upside down double 'Z'—all with his hands off the wheel, his arms wide like the bird that he was, controlling

The daring young man in his flying machine.

his machine with only his knees and torso. Wright had to concede Beachey's genius, as shown in this article from the *Dayton Journal,* August 2, 1914:

ORVILLE WRIGHT SAYS HE IS AMAZED AT ABILITY OF MAN HE TERMS WORLD'S GREATEST BIRDMAN

This is just an impression after seeing that wonderful Lincoln Beachey fly. It seems that Nature grew sorry because she did not endow this one man with wings and give him something else, brains, nerve, daring, courage, what you may, that even better with a mechanical contrivance than he ever could have hoped to fly with feathered members growing from his body. Nature has been a very merry jester with men, robbing them here to overpay there.

Others have seen this man Beachey in the air before he came to Dayton and they called him, "King of the Air." They said he was the most wonderful aviator in the world, that he defied death, and at the same time dared it and laughed at it and flirted with its grim spectre. But it did not seem to be any such thing yesterday when he amazed 30,000 people at the fairground in his wonderful, wonderful flights.

NO DANGERS FOR HIM

Really this man Beachey is in no danger at all. Is a pigeon, or a sparrow, or a gull or an albatross in danger when a-wing? Does one feel that the lark or the eagle or the sparrow is going to lose its equilibrium when hundreds of feet in the air and come toppling to the ground broken and bruised and dead?

No more does one feel fear for Lincoln Beachey. For he

knows how to fly, and knows how just as well as the birds know it. He is just as safe up there as they are and he can do things that they, poor things, never will do no matter how hard they try. He can fly faster than the fastest bird, the wild goose by more than twenty miles an hour; he can turn with the swiftness of a swallow, swoop with the suddenness of a hawk, and soar with more majesty than the eagle.

And though he is making a business of flying, Beachey seems to consider it nothing but play. No doubt he likes the sport of whirling through the air like some great buzzing, whirring, night bug, the singing motor sends him along at a speed that is marvelous and mystifying. Now he flies straightaway in a graceful sweep, but with ease he banks his machine and curves sharply to the right or left. Or ascends on a dizzy incline to glide downward at a sickening speed that, nevertheless, holds no dangers for him.

When Beachey flies, he flies. There is no fooling about it. He does not tinker and tinker and tinker with his aeroplane. The mechanicians have done all that, that's what he pays them for. He takes off his straw hat, brushes back his forehair, puts his flying hat on, turns his hat around, sits down in the chair with the belt about his body and then everybody gets out of the way.

Making his rise quickly, Beachey was hundreds of yards away, turning and swerving and swooping and climbing and doing everything that a bird could do, and some that no bird could do.

STRAIGHT FLYING PLEASES

What was announced as "straight flying" pleased the great mass of people better than anything else. The aviator did not go very high, choosing to remain near the ground, where the people could see him manipulate the machine that seemed to be a part of him.

Beachey passed in front of the grandstand and swooped down within a few feet of the ground, flying directly over the track. It was only when he flew close to the earth that a sensible idea of the tremendous speed was possible. He then turned upside-down then back, ascending up, up, up. At 5,000 feet Beachey deliberately turned his machine over on its back. But the motor kept on humming and forcing the aeroplane through the air. And he flew up-side-down and came back to the right position without the slightest difficulty.

Automobile horns, hands clapping and the shouts of admiring thousands greeted Beachey when he dropped down to the track and took the ground on a graceful glide. And the man who had done this wonderful thing in the air, hundreds of feet above the ground, put on his straw hat and walked away from his aircraft with now and then a bow to the throngs paying him homage.

But looping the loop was the principal thing the people wanted to see. They had heard of it and knew it to be a thing of reality but after all seeing is believing.

It was simple—for Beachey. He climbed again to a great height, to an almost vertical drop for several hundred feet and then started upon a gentle lift. His motor whirring steadily he held the plane so tilted and kept on going till the loop was completed. This time the people went wild with enthusiasm; they had seen him do it.

WRIGHT PAYS TRIBUTE

Orville Wright, celebrated as one of the pioneers of aeroplane aviation, paid Beachey a tribute on the track at the completion of his wonderful feats. Congratulating the aviator warmly upon the success of his achievements, Mr. Wright said: "Mr. Beachey, I consider you the most wonderful aviator the world yet has seen. Your performance has not only surprised me but it has amazed me as well."

Earlier he said to a reporter, "Beachey is more magnificent than I had imagined. I have watched him closely with my glasses and have never seen him make an error or falter. An aeroplane in the hands of Lincoln Beachey is poetry. His mastery is a thing of beauty to watch. He is the most wonderful flyer of all."

Another reporter asked Orville about Beachey's recklessness to which the aeroplane inventor replied, "He is apparently sensational and spectacular, but he is always safe. I studied him through my glasses, and when others have jumped to their feet in horror at what appeared to be an impending tragedy I have never feared for him. He knows what he is doing every minute of the time. To the spectators he is fearfully daring. He takes big chances. To the experts he is merely an intelligent, brainy, and heady operator, an ideal aviator."

AVIATOR FEARLESS

And when asked if he feared dying, Beachey thought for a moment, then looked up and said, "I know I am skillful: I have every confidence in my ability to combine thought and action to a degree sufficient to checkmate any treacherous trick of wind or weather. I am never afraid of myself. But I know as sure as fate that the day will come when there will be a tiny flaw in the piece of steel, just a little fleck, but it will not take longer than the tick of a watch; then it will be over." The aviator looked up at the reporters in awe of him and let a joke, "that is, if I stick to it forever. When I make a million, I'll quit."[6]

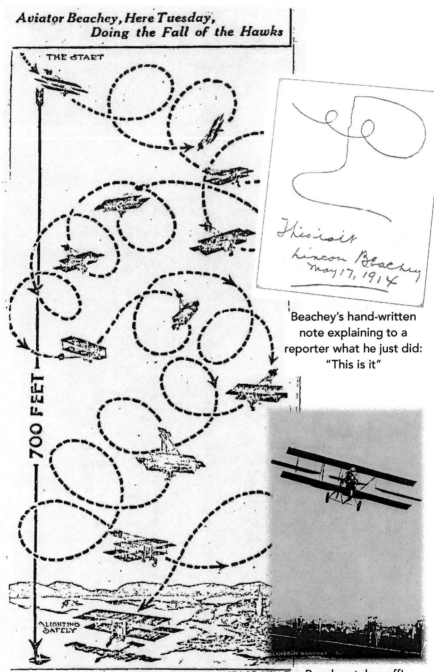

Aviator Beachey, Here Tuesday,
Doing the Fall of the Hawks

THE START

700 FEET

ALIGHTING SAFELY

Beachey's hand-written
note explaining to a
reporter what he just did:
"This is it"

Beachey completes a dozen loops
in the last 700 feet of his descent.

Beachey takes off!

187

The Genius Aviator in his newer and better flying machine.

Although few women writers in 1914 were given space in the newspapers, one female journalist was so impressed with Beachey's race against the famous automobilist that her lighthearted and humorous account of the race was featured in the Dayton papers.

WOMAN WRITER IS IMPRESSED BY MR. BEACHEY THE BIRD

What did you write to your mother at the lake, girls, after you went home from the fairgrounds yesterday afternoon?

Something like this maybe:

"Three of us were sitting in the shade west of the track with the wise one—or the ones that thought that they were wise. We sat on the grass and waited. Along came Barney Oldfield—going pretty fast. Then came the dust. Next time he came around he was faster yet, and the neat little racer ran up on the bank at the turn. One second after he passed, there was a stampede across the track. Nobody wanted Mr. Oldfield to get so close. Most of our wise friends were inside the ring now. We began to get lonely, and it looked as though there might be something doing over where it was sunny. We left the shade."

Beachey Goes Up

"Around by the automobile entrance they were wheeling out Mr. Beachey's little 700 lb. sensation maker. If there was ever anything prettier than the way it ran along and then lifted itself and sailed off over the heads of the 30,000, I'd like to see it. It was low flying. First a slant to one side, and then to the other—round and round the track. Then it whirred down and ran along and stopped, and everybody roared.

"Afterward he went up—way up—3,000 feet! You felt as if you were reading about the skylark in somebody's poem. And there was time to look at the sky and the light gray clouds that made a handsome background for Beachey the Bird—he will have to excuse the impertinence. Minutes and minutes went by and he kept going up, till he was almost too little to see.

"Then we suppose he acted according to a schedule—made a vertical drop of about 1,000 feet, attaining a speed of 200 miles an hour—and used the centrifugal force to throw the biplane on its back and flew upside-down for several seconds—picked out a landing spot while in the inverted position, made an upside-down spiral and righted the craft, dropping to his landing place with a dead motor.

"If he didn't do just that, it was something just as good. But wait. The best is yet to come.

"Beachey flew around the track, once, low down. He was getting ready to race with Oldfield for the earth and air championship. He passed the judges' stand a second time (by now, of course, we were just as near to the front row as we could get—standing on the running board of an unknown automobile in fact). Just as he passed there was a buzz on the track below him and there came Barney Oldfield in the little low car. Around they went. It made me think of the time the blue jay chased the cat that had robbed her nest. Beachey was just about that far above Oldfield. Beachey won easily.

"Then he looped the loop to end the show. You'll have to see that. It can't be compared to anything else that ever happened. Skylarks and blue jays were not in his class at all at that time. He probably did 'side-wise, backward handsprings, reverse loops, and regular loops' just as advertised. It looked wonderful. But he could have fooled most of us, I believe."

Half Were Women

"Then it was over. Short? Yes. Not more than an hour I should say. People had been there since twelve o'clock, they said, though the show began at three. They were ready to go—and he'd had the biggest show in years. We need more sport shows like this one. "Everybody was there. Promoters counted on thirty thousand and the crowd looked that size. Beachey played for a percentage of the gate and got $8,000 for the afternoon."

"Half of the crowd were women. One of them had a white-linen dress with a striped purple girdle and a purple tie and a purple hat with pink flowers, and purple stockings. She had dark hair and was probably the prettiest person there. A blonde woman wore a dull blue linen dress and carried a bright green parasol which sounds odd but looked rather nice. There were pale collars and vests and thins, and lots of vests in front. They have little pockets, you know, that you can put a street car ticket in—or a dime, if you have one.

Needless to say, it was a regular Dayton crowd. Good-natured to the limit and proud to death of being the home of the aeroplane."

Just Don't Know Why

'Why don't you go?' somebody said beforehand.

"We knew we were going but didn't know just why. We made up answers about looping the loop being a very useful feat in time of war.

"'When attacked by an enemy's aeroplane, the man that can loop the loop will be the man that makes good,' we explained.

"Our relatives, on the contrary, continued to insist that it was 'foolhardy,' 'unnecessary,' and other hard terms.

"Having been, however; we don't bother about explaining why we went. It was a good show—the best and shortest show that Dayton ever saw."[7]

The amused and highly personal tone of this piece, as well as the particular details recorded by the anonymous female journalist, show a marked difference from the many accounts written by men. Mr. Lincoln Beachey clearly had not lost his ability to charm the ladies.

Notes

1. Lincoln Beachey, pamphlet, "The Genius of Aviation," Courtesy San Diego Aerospace Museum.
2. Hans Christian Adamson, "The Man Who Owned the Sky" in *True Magazine*, February, 1953.
3. Hillery Beachey Collection, San Diego Aerospace Museum.
4. Adamson, Ibid.
5. Hillery Beachey Collection.
6. *Dayton Journal*, August 2, 1914
7. Ibid.

The Genius Aviator
...as the years fly by

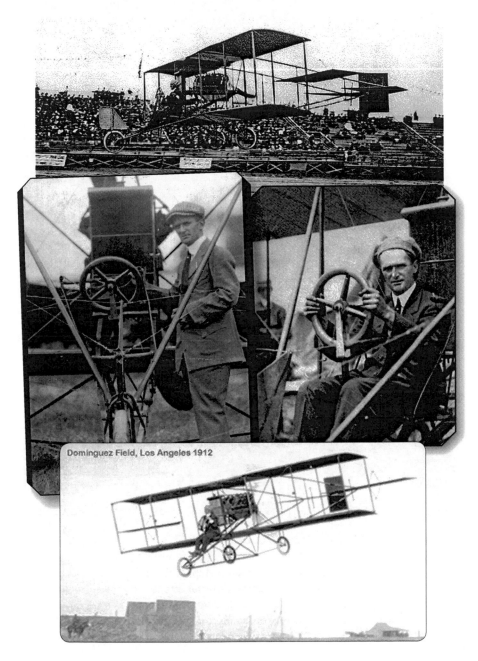

Dominguez Field, Los Angeles 1912

San Diego, November 26, 1914: Lincoln Beachey demonstrated the military use of airplanes by dropping sacks of flour on a ship, while Bill Pickens, his promotional wizard, set off charges to produce "special effects" of black smoke. Vast crowds and an armada of ships looked on in awe. The event was a fund-raiser for Belgium, which had just been invaded by Germany. This picture ran on the front page of the *San Diego Union*. *Courtesy San Diego Aerospace Museum*

A Force In the Air

I n the early days of exhibition flying after Dominguez, when flimsy machines and inexperienced pilots met with continued disaster, performances were often canceled due to wind and weather. Thousands who showed up to witness the mythic flying machines and were disappointed raised a cry of fakery and revenge. To counter the mood of hesitation and disbelief that still surrounded the new field of aeronautics, Beachey's advertisements guaranteed a performance and carried his slogan, "Rain, Shine, or Cyclone." He put all doubts to rest indeed, when he flew in the face of a lightning storm:

> "This is the Life" broke out the band as Beachey started his first ascent. With lightning breaking through the clouds all around him, the daring young aviator reached an altitude of 3,000 feet, and braving the electrical storm, gave an astounding exhibition of the exploits which have made him the greatest birdman of the twentieth century.
>
> As he zoomed past the grandstands, the band struck up "Too Much Mustard" and every person in the stands appeared to sway with him as he fearlessly danced and "tangoed" just a few feet above the ground.[1]

On September 25, 1914, in Springfield, Illinois, Lincoln got the telegram he had long waited for: the Secretaries of the Army and Navy invited him to come to Washington and demonstrate the aeroplane for them. He wired his acceptance and indicated he would come immediately. Lincoln canceled his next day's show, <u>the only cancellation of his career</u>, and traveled through the night to the nation's Capitol. Lincoln showed up at the Department of Defense the next day, but only two Secretaries and aides were there. "Where are the Congressmen, where's the President?" Lincoln asked.

The Secretaries explained, "Congress is in session, and the President is working in the White House, but you are to show us your demonstration and then we will take that information to them."

Lincoln had not traveled and campaigned across the whole country for a demonstration for two Cabinet members. Lincoln had broken the rules here before: it was time to do it again.

Legend has it that President Wilson was work-ing on neutrality papers in the Oval Office when he heard what he thought was a fly. Picking up his swatter, he began to stalk the intruder. But the buzzing got louder and appeared to be coming from outside. Wilson looked out his window and saw, heading for the windows of the Oval Office like an arrow for a bull's eye, an 800 pound biplane with the pilot out front staring directly at him. Wilson broke into a sweat when

President Wilson in the White House

he and the pilot could see each other quite clearly and the plane did not waver from its deadly course. At the last possible moment, Lincoln pulled his machine straight up and spun his machine, flashing his name written across the wings, B-E-A-C-H-E-Y. The birdman climbed above the White House, looped back and dived at it again and again as if on a devastating bombing run. The crowds formed everywhere below, filling the Mall, arresting the entire town.

Lincoln quickly refueled, climbed, and dived toward the Mall,

Enormous crowds filled the Capitol Mall to watch Beachey fly upside down past the Washington Monument. *Courtesy San Diego Aerospace Museum*

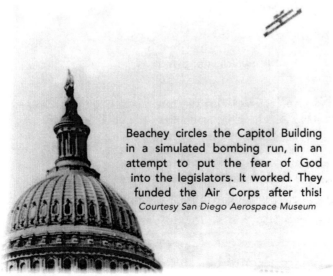

Beachey circles the Capitol Building in a simulated bombing run, in an attempt to put the fear of God into the legislators. It worked. They funded the Air Corps after this! *Courtesy San Diego Aerospace Museum*

pulled up just a scant 100 feet above the amazed onlookers, flipped his machine over and flew upside down past the Washington Monument. Every set of eyes was fixed upwards to see written upon his top wing what the President had read, B-E-A-C-H-E-Y, as he shot like a lightning bolt across the sky, headed straight for the Capitol.

He was determined that every legislator would see the genius of aviation, and know the power of the aeroplane.

Congress adjourned to witness the spectacle. Lincoln attacked the capitol again and again as if on a bombing run, and ended his flight by waving his wings to Congress. The lawmen cheered him as he flew back to the polo field across from the White

AFTER WATCHING MONDAY'S TWISTERS.

Newspaper cartoonists had a field day after Beachey buzzed the Capitol Building and White House in Washington. The stunt made news all over the country.

Courtesy San Diego Aerospace Museum

House. Again he quickly refueled and climbed to 3000 feet and performed another aerial ballet for the throngs. Suddenly, he seemed to be stuck upside down, and worse, his motor quit and he began to fall and spin! He dropped out of the sky in a deadly upside-down spiral, and from a distance, did not seem to pull out of it. Personnel at the

Army hospital saw the aviator fall and rushed out with ambulances. Telegraph operators also witnessed the out of control plummet and instantly tapped out the news to the nation: Lincoln Beachey was dead!

At the polo field Secretary Daniels was congratulating Lincoln when they heard someone yelling, "Make way, move aside," and saw the crowds parting. The Army medics broke into the open surrounding the aeroplane, looked frantically in all directions and asked in confusion, "Where's the crash?"

Beachey smiled and asked, "What crash?"

The medics were dumbfounded at the crowd's seeming lack of concern: "We saw a plane crash over here!"

Beachey feigned insult. "That was no crash," he said, proudly putting his hands on his hips. "I always land that way."

Later when he spoke to the President and assembled Congressmen, he said, "If I had had a bomb, you would be dead. You were defenseless. It is time to put a force in the air."[2]

Beachey shakes hands with the Secretary of War and other Cabinet members after giving them the thrill of a lifetime.

The editors of *Aero and Hydro*, the country's leading voice of American aviation, lauded Beachey's aerial demonstration as an heroic act which had forced the government to recognize the necessity of their involvement in the new technology of aviation.

AMERICA'S AVIATION WEEKLY

While Beachey's flights were unofficially "official," Aero and Hydro cannot but believe that American aviation has been given a distinct impetus that will be incalculable in its benefits. Such a forceful and practical demonstration before the Members of our Congress cannot fail of great good to all directly or indirectly concerned in our great aeronautic movement and we venture the prediction that its future stability is marked from this event.

When the heads of the fighting men of the country and their staffs, and the Senators and Congressmen exhibit the enthusiasm we could not help but witness after the flights, when the Capitol is set all agog on the subject of aviation and evidences of greater Military and Naval aero activity immediately blossom forth, we cannot help but extend our best congratulations to Lincoln Beachey, "the agnostic of rational flying," so often falsely decried as a distinct menace to the science of flight, on his brilliant work and his magnanimous co-operation in this effort to wake up the country to things aviatic and create a demand for meritorious "made-in-America" aeronautic products.[3]

Many lawmakers sent expressions of gratitude to Lincoln for opening their eyes to the development of air power. Congress proposed that San Francisco be the site of the first governmental aero post in America under the direction of California's premier aviator. Lincoln was honored by the proposal, but having already committed himself to headlining the upcoming World's Fair, he postponed taking up the position for another year. Still, the die was cast, and Congress finally began appropriating significant dollars to the creation of an air force.

The cynics who for years had called Lincoln "crazy" and "dangerous" were silenced by the government's recognition of his aeronautical genius. Many of the country's top aviators endorsed Beachey's stalwart leadership, and newspaper editorials everywhere no longer questioned his "antics" but gave unparalleled accolades to the master of the air. An editorial from *The St. Louis Gazette* summarized the public's sentiment toward America's most popular hero:

> When a person talks aviation or aviators, 90 people out of every 100 instinctively say, "You know I saw Beachey at such and such place?" or "Did you ever see Beachey fly?" Why is it that Beachey is unique in being uppermost in the minds of everyone whom sky flying is talked of? Why is it today that Beachey is the only aviator in North America who can play any type of city or town, and unaided, pack the parks and tracks and grandstands to suffocation?
>
> The principal reason that Lincoln Beachey is to aviation what Marshall Field's is to the dry goods trade, what the Imperator is to the shipping world, what Richard Mansfield was to the American dramatic stage. He is the big, central figure. In the esteem of the public he stands alone.
>
> A serious accident to Beachey would wound the people of America more deeply than Beachey would be hurt. There is genuine affection for him in the hearts of the

American people. He is our standard, as far as aviation is concerned. Long may he wave.

People no longer hold up Wright or Curtiss as examples of greatness in the mastery of the sky.

This is a Beachey Age.

If Lincoln Beachey was flying from one park and twenty-four other aviators were flying in unison in a park across the street, the public would flock to see Beachey perform. It has been proven time and time again.

Beachey did not achieve his present prominence or vogue without the hardest kind of struggle. He served a cold apprenticeship. But he was brave, unassuming, persistent. He was both a dreamer and a realist. He dreamed the "loop" five years ago and when he told Glenn Curtiss and Bleriot and the other world figures of aviation of his ideas they laughed at him. Then, Pegoud, at Marseilles, France, performed the "loop" and astonished the scientific world. Out of his retirement came Beachey and in four months he not only turned the first "loop" in America, but did Pegoud 'one better'. Then he perfected his "death drop," falling from the clouds from 5,000 feet with a dead motor, throwing the machine over and flying upside-down. It took him three months to perfect the "death drop." In that three months he could have filled his purse by playing two scores of exhibitions and depending on his trick flying and "looping" for drawing cards.

But Beachey does not figure time or money as opposed to being in a class by himself. He stayed at the San Diego Aviation field for months and perfected this drop, and when he came east last May he was in a position to present a program which since that time has thrilled millions all over the eastern states, and which has more firmly than ever established him as the greatest aviator the world has ever known.[4]

BEACHEY
Flies Upside Down
Every Day
Rain or Shine

BROCKTON
FAIR

SEPT. 29, 30 – OCT. 1, 2 1914

The very next day after his Washington stunts, Beachey was in Massachusetts for an exhibition when the crowds broke through barricades as he was landing and rushed onto the field to carry him away. Beachey had to crash his plane into a fence in order to avoid hitting people. He was unhurt.

Courtesy San Diego Aerospace Museum

cross the San Francisco bay, the football rivalry between the University of California at Berkeley and Stanford University in Palo Alto had already been established. No matter who else they played, the biggest game each year was between these two powerhouses for the honor of hosting the Stanford Axe for a year. The contest was not limited to the gridiron, however, as the schools tried to outdo each other with some kind of crazy stunt or wild antic outside the football game as well.

Unbeknownst to the Cal Bears, the Stanford (then) Indians hired none other than Lincoln Beachey to fly into the Berkeley Stadium dressed in Stanford Crimson: a bright Stanford sweater with a giant "S" on the front and a cape. Beachey dived at the Berkeley cheering section and threw a crimson football like a bomb to the ground. He landed and strode amid college cheers into the Cal Bear bleachers. This "bombing run" deeply impressed one particular student in the stands that fateful day, and the power of the aeroplane became the focus of the mind of young Curtiss LeMay, who is referred to as 'The Father of Strategic Bombing'.

Stanford had won the off field battle and, using this momentum, went on to win the football game as well.

A young
Curtiss LeMay

incoln was close to realizing all of his dreams. The 126-city glory tour had a tremendous effect upon the nation. Washington began to act, people clamored for flying, and aviation was given its direly needed shot in the arm. He was "known by sight to hundreds of thousands and by name to the whole world." He returned triumphantly to San Francisco to demonstrate the pinnacle of man's achievement at the World's Fair. Now the world would come to him, and the tribulations of road life would be over. Settled in his love of Merced, settled into fame, settled with death, he settled down in San Francisco.

He would be the daily headliner at the world's fair, and he learned that he would be awarded a gold medal by the participating nations for his contributions to the art and science of flying. They would finally acknowledge that indeed he was the unrivaled genius of aviation.

Warren Eaton, Beachey's mechanician and co-designer, appears to be scolding Beachey before take-off in the Little Looper.

Courtesy San Diego Aerospace Museum

Notes

1, Unidentified newspaper clipping in the Hillery Beachey Collection, San Diego Aerospace Museum.

2. Hans Christian Adamson, "The Man Who Owned the Sky" in *True Magazine*, February, 1953.

3. *Aero and Hydro*, October 3 1914.

4. Hillery Beachey Collection.

Merced Walton ♥ A True Match

Merced Walton brought a new kind of promise to Lincoln Beachey's life in 1914.

16

A Feeling Like Love

With Europe falling into war, America became the focus of international tourism. A party for the entire world was going on in San Francisco, and of course, San Francisco knows how to throw a party. The celebration was historically described as "the last fling of naïve idealism," and for good reason.

San Francisco's newest City Hall was the crown jewel in this phoenix-city of jewels. Lincoln Beachey had been selected as the Master of Ceremonies for its opening. But with the Fair preparations and his new monoplane design, he was suddenly too busy to participate in this half-day ceremony. However, he personally delivered the Master of Ceremony papers to the up-and-coming, sensational

Due to his
obligations at the
Fair, Lincoln as Master
of Ceremonies hands the honor
of opening San Francisco's new City Hall
to up-and-coming star, Charlie Chaplin.

Charlie Chaplin, together with Edna
Purviance, who was filming *A Jitney
Elopement in Golden Gate Park.*

The World's Fair was described as "a seething surging mass of humanity all bent on having a good time"[1] trying to forget the tension
growing in Europe. Only England and Germany did not send representatives to the Fair—they would not share the same ground—but
both sent exhibits. The pall of war gave the Fair an edge of desperation.

The Panama-Pacific International Exposition was "an ideal city
within an ideal city,"[2] rivaling Renaissance Venice or ancient Athens.
The marshy area below Cow Hollow had been transformed utterly
into a brilliant fairyland three miles long and a half a mile wide. Ford,

Edison and Burbank had worked their magic upon the celebration. In addition to overseeing all the Fair's machinery, Ford also ran a working assembly line, producing cars daily at the Expo; the entire Exposition was laid out around six large gardens overflowing with Burbank's splendor; and lighting the night sky was Edison's Scintillator—49 of the world's first incandescent spotlights painting pastel streaks across the evening fog, simulating the Aurora Borealis, and splashing the Tower of Jewels with dancing colors. If the famous San Francisco fog rolled through the Golden Gate, it was a spectacle not to be missed.

The two most treasured buildings of the Fair were the Palace of Fine Arts and the Tower of Jewels. The Palace of Fine Arts stood at the western edge of the Fairgrounds proper and was of Greek and Roman architecture; its reconstruction stands today. Simulating the setting

Thousands of people gathered daily to watch Lincoln Beachey take off on his
3 p.m. flight at the 1915 Panama-Pacific International Exhibition. Thick fog
obscures the Expo buildings in the background.
Courtesy San Diego Aerospace Museum

sun, it was crowned by a pastel orange dome and stood like a jewel
upon some grand Jeweler's setting, and embraced by a semi-circle of
colonnades 1100 feet around the perimeter. Inside, twenty eight countries presented their nations' finest works. 11,000 pieces of the world's
finest art were assembled within the Palace, and chiffoned maidens
danced in boats upon the lagoon surrounding it. The celebration of
beauty was something like heaven, but only something like it. For gigantic maidens stood along the top of the colonnades, but all turned

in, with heads low; they were crying that the fullness of divine beauty cannot be represented.

Standing two thirds the height of the Eiffel Tower, the Tower of Jewels stood at the Fair's center, covered with 125,000 separate jew-

els, like the crystals on fine chandeliers. Each crystal hung by a thread from a silver post, backed by its own mirror, and rocked in the wind. Gazing upon the Tower of Jewels was like being taken by sunlight dancing upon the water. In rapt contemplations, every

breath of wind could be seen in sparkling rainbows racing across the tower like waves across a wheat field.

There were forty-seven miles of walkways on the Fair site, and if one spent just two and a half minutes at each exhibit or activity, it would take over one year to see it all. A special club was formed by runners who had traversed every pathway. The world's largest amusement park, The Zone, thrilled children of all ages, and on the stage, the worlds finest artists performed, including Loie Fuller's dance troupe, Ignacy Paderewski, Charlie Chaplin, and John Phillip Sousa.

The Palace of Machinery, the world's largest framed structure where Beachey had flown inside during construction, held a wondrous collection of human inventions. Beginning with arrowheads and stone age tools, the exhibit progressed through the ages (Guttenberg's Press was brought), and ended with the pinnacle of technological achievement, the quintessential invention: Lincoln Beachey's Little Looper. Every day, at three o'clock, the giant doors of the Palace of Machinery would open, and the world's greatest aviator and hometown hero would fly the world's greatest invention as history's daily high point. The idealism was so thick, you hoped beyond hope that it wouldn't break.

The opening of the fair was indeed electrifying. A quarter of a million people gathered around the Fountain of Energy for the opening celebration. At twelve o'clock high, after welcoming addresses by Governor Hiram Johnson and Mayor "Sunny" Jim Rolph, President Wilson hit a telegraph switch in *Washington, D.C.* and the fountain sprang alive!

Lincoln Beachey gazed down upon the fair high amongst cumulus clouds, unbeknownst to the crowds. When he saw the fountain spring to life, he knew it was his time. Lincoln turned to the four birds in a cage next to him and reassured them, "Hang on guys, here we go," and dropped like a sudden meteor from the heavens directly toward the Fair's center.

Soon the shrill of his machine captured everyone's attention as Beachey plummeted towards the Fountain's center. The San Francisco *Examiner* described the event:

San Francisco Examiner
Monarch of the Dailies

VAST CROWD IS THRILLED BY AVIATOR

Far above the great crowds which flowed through the avenues of the Exposition, in alternating sun and rain and hail, Lincoln Beachey, the aviator, spun a pathway of white smoke yesterday afternoon, as he circled above the Tower of Jewels, shortly after the official opening of the Exposition.

Beachey enjoyed that flight. He looked down, he said, upon the greatest crowd he had ever seen. And he has flown all over the world.

He was the only one who saw the entire crowd in a bird's-eye view. Every street, he said, and every open space, was black with people.

Releases four white doves

As he shot out from the sky, all other objects lost interest, for the moment, to the Exposition visitors.

The guns had just done booming, and the fountains had been set in motion.

Just five hundred feet above the Tower of the Jewels, Beachey released four white doves from a cage. They dropped, and then spread their wings, and sailed over the buildings, emblematic of the spirit of peace brooding there.

Then Beachey gave the people a great thrill, He performed the upside-down loop for which he is famous, in three great loops. Barely had he righted from one loop than he swung into another.

It seemed that he would fall straight down upon the buildings, that he had lost control, that his engine had broken or wing snapped.

All these sensations thrilled the crowd in the brief time

that the aviator hung head down like a wounded bird, but he always arose again.

The flight added the last touch of beauty to the scene. As its engine spat out smoke in its swift drive, the curves formed by his evolutions remained outlined in fairy colors. His loop the loop left a great circle in the sky, white against a perfect blue, with machine and driver a twisting black fantasy.[3]

Merced and Lincoln walked the Fair arm in arm, "Mr. Pan Pacific" and his fiancée, or along from the Cliff House at the end of Geary and down to Lincoln's hangar in the nearby dunes. Everywhere they walked, people were kind and did not ask for autographs nor point too loudly. They had dinner with mom, lunch with the mayor. They talked of their future, of children's names, and aviation. They looked forward to their marriage in June.

To Lincoln, his hangar at the beach was the beginning of Lincoln Beachey Aviation, manufacturer of high-performance aeroplanes. Warren Eaton, designer and builder of the Little Looper, headed a devoted crew, including Hillery. Their prototype was a sleek, high-powered monoplane. Monoplanes had always impressed Lincoln, beaten him on occasion. Their fragility, however, kept them out of Lincoln's hands. Until now.

Warren, Hillery, and crew had assembled a beautiful machine under Lincoln's direction. Poised on a tricycle undercarriage, her slender cream fuselage and lovely yellow wings sweeping out from her midsection spelled speed. Because of the enclosed cockpit and with just one expanse of wing, the lines of the plane suggested an elegant bird. Eaton had constructed the machine similar to the European monoplanes with their "taube" (dove) design. The ailerons were put at the ends and rear of the wings and, like the elevators and tail, were oversized for exaggerated aerobatic control. The wings were given extra strength for inverted

Beachey's new monoplane schematic drawings and pilot in cockpit, 1915.

stress with support wires running below to the tricycle landing gear. Above the fuselage corresponding wires ran to the top of a pipe pyramid that provided additional support from above the wings.

Out front, the smooth, circular cowling around the Gnome motor was the final aerodynamic touch—and castor oil protector. The most distinctive feature of the monoplane, as opposed to his Little Looper 'pusher', was that the pilot sat *in* the fuselage, *behind* the motor, unfortunately in line with hot oil which spewed freely from the rotating Gnome. A small, tilted windshield was installed on the fuselage directly

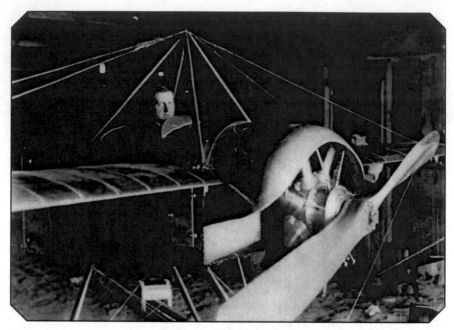

Beachey sits in his new monoplane, the Taube (Dove), in his hangar at Ocean Beach, San Francisco. The aerodynamic cowl over the motor helped keep the caster oil from spewing out into the pilot's face. The "pyramid" of cables over the cockpit was intended to stabilize the wings. *Courtesy Hud Weeks Collection*

in front of the cockpit, but Lincoln would have to give up his three piece suit and instead wear a flying suit, goggles, and helmet. Enclosed in a cockpit, Lincoln would not be as sensitive to the pressures and feeling of the wind and weather. But it was worth it: the new machine was as light and strong and sleek as the materials of the time would allow.

Lincoln began putting the new plane through speed and maneuverability trials. He clocked in at 105 miles per hour on a straight and level course above the beach—*20* miles per hour faster than he had gone in his two-winged Pusher.

When the Fair Officials saw Lincoln's Taube, they pleaded with him to fly it on "Beachey Day", where he would be the focus of honor. Even with the perfect bait, Lincoln declined; the plane was brand new and had not been really tested. He promised, however, to consider it.

Beachey was unhappy with the helmet and other gear
he had to wear in order to fly the new monoplane.
Courtesy Hud Weeks Collection

Warren Eaton and Beachey prepare the new plane for take-off on the
hard sand at Ocean Beachey. The tricycle landing gear was tied with
wires to the wings to provide strength for aerobatic stresses.
Courtesy Hud Weeks Collection

March 3rd, 1915, was Lincoln Beachey's twenty-eighth birthday, and the day the Fair anticipated its one-millionth visitor. But to Lincoln, the most important person was his mother, Amy. He escorted her to the top of the Tower of Jewels, left her there with an escort, and went to the Little Looper for his three o'clock show. Dropping and looping six consecutive times in front of his mother in the Tower, he wrote 1-0-0-0-0-0-0 in the sky, using smoke from his motor,

The Tower of Jewels

then he flew a full aerial performance. Mother and son blew kisses to each other as Lincoln finished his ride. The crowds may have enjoyed a magnificent performance, but the show was for her alone.

"1-0-0-0-0-0-0" — Beachey's plane did a dive and six loops to celebrate the one-millionth visitor at the 1915 World's Fair, but really was just for his mom.

So many people asked Lincoln what it was like to fly, he wrote an article for his hometown paper, The *San Francisco Chronicle*. In an age when reading and writing reigned supreme, even a middle-school drop-out could craft a literary expression.

San Francisco Chronicle

LOOPING THE LOOP OVER THE EXPOSITION

It had been foggy, but when I went up the clouds were breaking. Now and then there were rifts of blue sky in between, although they closed right up again. Corporal Mix was tuning up the motor. Then I jumped into the seat. Mix and Eaton, my other mechanician, gave the propeller a twist, and away I shot down the sandy beach like a swallow. Then I pulled back on the wheel.

That is an advantage of these light machines—you can start up almost immediately. My Looper has only a twenty-four foot spread, and it weighs seven hundred pounds. It is the lightest biplane I have ever seen, although this new monoplane here will weigh more than 200 pounds less, and will have just a twenty-foot spread of wings.

I shot up at a good stiff angle. And then I saw that I was going right into that cloud bank, which was a pity, because the beach down there and the exposition roads were black with people who had come to see the stunts. Then I hit the mist. An instant later I could have shot through that mist blanket and I could have sung out loud for pure joy.

It was blue up there—blue! The sun was streaming down like so much golden champagne. The bluer hills outlined the Golden Gate perfectly, and the clouds themselves were a great billowy ocean that had filled up the basin of San Francisco Bay. The underside of a cloudy sky is always gray and cheerless, but the topside is the whitest foamiest thing you ever saw. But the drifts of mist were already breaking up rapidly, and so I began to see the city and the hills and the exposition buildings below in little glimpses.

A SWIRLING FUNNEL OF AIR

The fog, you might say, had been punched full of holes. These holes in the fog were peculiar that winter's day! Each one had a swirling funnel of air pouring down into it. The holes themselves kept moving and closing and opening up again, and I had to hold the wheel delicately as I rose over.

Sooner or later the fog would be wiped out completely, and I had a programme of stunts to pull off. But for the moment I just rode around over that mist ocean, and leaned a little to the right or left, and made a few figure eights over the exposition site while the holes underneath me grew bigger and bigger.

So that is how I saw the exposition, and I suppose you want to know how it looked.

Those wonderful domes and roofs, green and blue and white, and tossing back the coquetting sunshine, were just a great collection of beautiful soap bubbles.

Of course, the exposition is laid out with great formality—so many gardens here, and so many transepts there, and a court on this side of the Tower of Jewels, flanking a court on that—but it was not the sort of formality, as I stared down at it—that wearies the eye.

Not at all. The gardens and domes and the pastel colors that have been applied to those domes and walls, offer variety of a thousand kinds.

As a matter of fact, those buildings are very lofty, as buildings go—some of them fifty feet or more. But there are acres and acres of them, and from us aloft they just seem to flatten right into the lawns and trees. A building several stories high does not represent much in altitude to an aviator whose day's programme is to include an ascension to 10,000 feet.

But to the architects of this exposition I want to pay

one compliment. They have provided an exposition whose roofs are just as beautiful as its walls. The roofs of the exhibit palaces, the golden dome of the Massachusetts State Building, the columns and arches and shimmering cut glass facets of the Tower of Jewels, are indescribably beautiful to one who looks down from the air, just as they are to one who looks down from the crest of San Francisco's surrounding hills. I speak with some authority about this. I suppose I have seen my share of roofs.

All this while the people were gazing up from the grandstands and the sandy beach below. I remembered that I had not come there just to be an overhead tourist.

So I flew down then over the heads of the people that blackened the Esplanade. I took my hands off the wheel and waved them out at my side, and they shouted at me. I shot off again, down the length of the beach to the California building, and pulled the wheel back as far as I dared. Bill Pickens, my manager, says that I went straight up for about ten miles. It was really only about 2,000 feet.

COMPLIMENTS ARCHITECTS

I threw my shoulder to the right, and around she circled with a big teeter. Then I headed down that air lane with the funny-looking, incongruous jumble of columns and minarets of the Zone below me. The motor was roaring in my ears like the surf. I pushed the wheel forward an inch or two and down we went. Then when the momentum was good and terrific, I pulled her back again, and over we went like a pinwheel, with my head in the center.

As soon as the machine righted, I took another straight shoot, pointed her down again, did a loop, and flew forward. I had to swing to the left to keep within sight of the crowd, and after the fifth loop I was looking right down on Alcatraz Island, I flew over it quite low. There was a corral full of Government mules down there, who heard my motor and thought I was some kind of a horse-fly such as they never had dreamed of. I wish you could have seen the stampede among those Government mules.

After that I wheeled back, glad that the clouds were all brushed out of the sky, and pointed her up until we were somewhere around 5,000 feet.

It was my plan to tilt the machine down until it was pointed straight at that Tower of Jewels, and then do what Bill advertises as the "death dip."

The "death dip" calls for the straightest sort of a shoot downward, so that people will think you are falling. Then with a quick twist of the wheel you go sailing off over their heads, just as they have begun to shiver and grow faint, and you have a good laugh at them.

I took a good grip on the wheel and pushed her over, and for a few fractions of seconds I was slipping down the air faster than men have ever done since Darius Green made his melancholy demonstration.

The way that Tower of Jewels moved its flagpole up toward me was enough to make me think this monument and the whole exposition was trying to move up toward me and embrace me with its courts and gardens.

I flew over to my landing place for the oxygen tank then, and stepped down a minute. It was in the scheme of things to try for an altitude record.

A moment later I climbed back into the seat. In my little biplane the driver's seat is away forward, to give the machine its proper balance. This is a particularly danger-ous place for an operator to sit, because even the slight-est accident—such as misjudging your landing place and bumping into a fence—will bring the entire motor crush-ing into you by its own momentum.

The boys spun the propeller for me again, and I shot up. Now I want to describe what I saw as clearly as possible, because I really took time to enjoy a good look at California's wonderful exposition and San Francisco, too—with her bay and her hills and valleys. By this time the sky had nicely opened up.

Beneath me the great golden dome of the Massachusetts State Building was the one conspicuous object.

As the fair buildings and the gardens, and then the whole circling city fell farther and farther away, it began to grow good and chilly. San Francisco's winter climate is just as frosty as any on earth, if you try it high enough.

But this was an unusual day. The city and all those islands in the bay were just as clear now as if I were moving over them with a telescope. The whole of the great big Northern California was opening out under me like a relief map. This Mount Tamalpais, across the Golden Gate, is about 2500 feet high, and presently I was looking away down on it. I judged that I had climbed about 5,000 feet, but still I spiraled up and up and I was mighty glad of a leather coat and all those sweaters.

AN ALTITUDE OF 10,000 FEET

When the time eventually came for my motor to cease pushing me upward I had registered considerably over 10,000 feet, but a 700-pound biplane is not fitted for altitude records. It was then, at the very "peak" of my career, as you might say, that I determined to push my monoplane to completion as fast as possible. With its 490 pounds weight and its wonderful elasticity in the air—it will have the smallest wing spread that I have ever used on any aircraft—I feel certain of my ability to top all altitudes.

I rode on the highest level of air I have ever attained, making free use of my oxygen tank, and up there I saw the sun go down into the ocean beyond the Golden Gate.

Hillery Beachey poured his talent into the design of the beautiful new Taube.
Here the rear section of the fuselage has not yet been covered over.
Courtesy Hud Weeks Collection

It fell into the sea like a great red orange, and all the sky and ocean were painted with it. The Sierra, 200 miles to the east, came out distinctly in the evening shadow. It was very cold, and I blew upon my hands, first one and then the other, as I cruised about in the sunset under circumstances that I know have never been experienced before on this particular edge of the continent.

Then I swept down in long, easy undulations that carried me first to Goat Island and then back to Fort Point, and still I was high over the city. As I descended some of that last sunshine broke on the glass dome of the Palace of Horticulture and turned it into a livid pyre.

For the last few hundred feet I did a quick volplane and landed in a meadow picked out for my purposes, and when I got out I was very stiff.[4]

Lincoln Beachey and Warren Eaton pose with their new pride and joy
on the sands of Ocean Beach below San Francisco's famed Cliff House.
Courtesy Hud Weeks Collection

Lincoln Beachey was at the peak of American adoration, and was larger than life to the common person. A glimpse of the regard he enjoyed can easily be seen by the deference and awe two reporters showed him when he granted them a personal interview.

EXCLUSIVE INTERVIEW WITH THE BIRDMAN

Keep your seats, friends; we are going to have a heart to heart talk with Lincoln Beachey, the greatest aviator the world has ever known.

Beachey sat alone in his mother's modest home, and it was with considerable shyness that we entered the presence of this great man. We had heard so much about him, about his wonderful flying, his daring feats, his death-defying stunts in the air, that we almost imagined he would be far from an ordinary man. But he wasn't. He was just a plain, everyday sort of man, of common tastes, and thinks he is no better than anyone else. And he smokes

The Taube is still unfinished in this picture: Warren Eaton strides away as Lincoln ponders his creation. The aileron portions of the wings and the elevators on the tail are oversized for extra aerobatic control. The plane was a cream-yellow color.
Courtesy Hud Weeks Collection

5 cent cigars which retail at only one jitney apiece! We could hardly believe it, but he showed us the brand. They were—-well, no free advertising for any cigar firm, but we assure you they were 5-cent cigars.

Beachey is short of stature, but by no means bad looking, and with a smile and a hearty handshake that would put an office-seeking candidate in the shade.

He extended his hand and we grasped it. "I'm certainly glad to meet you," he said. "Won't you sit down?"

We accepted the invitation and proceeded to look the great man over. He smiled at our apparent display of awe.

"Now I want you to feel right at home," said Beachey. "Here, have a smoke and tell me just what you want. I'll be glad to give you any information you may desire."

We accepted the smoke with considerable alacrity.

Cigars are somewhat of a luxury to a poor newspaper man, who, as a general rule, can smoke nothing better than a pipe, and we were about to light it when we were struck with a bright idea. At times an idea really does strike us, and this was one of those times. Why smoke this cigar? Had it not been presented to us by a truly great man? Therefore, was it not a fitting keepsake? Indeed it was, and so we stored it carefully in an outside pocket, and it will repose for years to come with other relics we have gathered in past years.

Finally we mustered up sufficient courage to speak. "Well, Mr. Beachey, our readers would like to know how it feels to soar up into the clouds."

"All I can say is that I like it," said Beachey.

"What! Do you mean to say, Mr. Beachey, that there is any pleasure in such a display of recklessness?" We could hardly believe our ears.

Again that broad smile flitted across his features, and somehow we felt more at ease. "Call it what you like, my friend, but don't call it recklessness. Yes, indeed I like it. I am always careful. I always thoroughly overhaul my machine before every flight, examine every wire, test the engine, and get everything into shape so that there is practically no danger. No, I am not reckless, as many people believe."

We took his word for it. "How does it feel, Mr Beachey, to fly thousands of feet in the air in this manner?"

"Well, it is a pleasing sensation that I cannot describe. You know when a man's in love? A feeling something like that."

"Is it that pleasing?" we exclaimed. And right then and there we decided that flying must be all right.

"You see, there is always a chance that you might fall; you are always in some danger, just the same as when you are in love. That's why I make the comparison. Many an aviator has taken a hard fall, never to recover—and so has many a lover.

"A great scientist once told me that I had the bird instinct in my being. As a boy, I was a great lover of birds. Their song did not appeal to me as much as their superb dips and dives and other feats of flying. I often wanted to emulate them. Now I can do things the birds cannot do. I can loop the loop and fly upside-down.

"You ask me how it feels," continued the great aviator, "to soar in the heavens. Well, as you go up, up, up, you seem to be standing still with the earth rapidly moving away from you. And as you mount higher the air becomes cooler. Far below you can see the world stretched beneath, and the cities look like toy houses, the people look like midgets. It is a pleasing sensation; makes one feel free and happy and helps to drive away your earthly troubles.

"It is simply the dancing along life's icy brink and the attendant excitement that makes life worth while. Chance-taking is not a business with me. It is a delightful diversion, and no music lover ever is more charmed by listening to the inspiring strains of his favorite opera, superbly sung by a great artist, than I am charmed by the hum of my motor when I am sailing in or out of a loop and upside-down flight. Some hunt lions and tigers for thrills. But I love the sky and answer its call because my whole life centers around the sensations of flying."[5]

Notes

1. *The Color Handbook of the Panama Pacific International Exposition*, 1915, private collection.
2. Panama Pacific International Exposition promotional brochure, private collection.
3. San Francisco *Examiner*, February 20, 1915.
4. Unidentified San Francisco newspaper clipping.
5. Unidentified newspaper clipping in the Hillery Beachey collection, San Diego Aerospace Museum.

"The World's Greatest Aviator," "Alexander of the Air,"
the "Divine Flyer" prepares to take off.

A publicity portrait shows the diamond stickpin Lincoln always wore, even when he was flying. *Courtesy San Diego Aerospace Museum*

"A Show They'll Never Forget"

L incoln was satisfied with his tests of the monoplane. In his hands, it evoked the elegance of a flying dove. On Friday afternoon, March 12, 1915, two days before his gold medal award ceremony, he looped his 'Taube' in two graceful circles, and spun her like a top going across the Fairgrounds. Then he decided he would yield to the Fair officials and fly the monoplane for "Beachey Day".

Sunday finally came. Lincoln had hardly slept. Soon, the nations of the world would celebrate his contributions to aviation—in his hometown. The honor was beyond belief, and Lincoln was overwhelmed. Getting into his white roadster, he kissed Merced goodbye. She stayed behind with Beachey's mother at Frank Carroll's home to put together the post-award celebration.

PRESENTED TO
LINCOLN BEACHEY
ON THE TENTH ANNIVERSARY
OF HIS FIRST FLIGHT
IN APPRECIATION OF HIS SKILL,
COURAGE AND LOYAL SERVICE
TO THE EXPOSITION
AND SAN FRANCISCO.
MARCH 14, 1915

The Exposition grounds were packed with fifty thousand people, while five times that many crowded o u t s i d e the Fairground; every open space was packed going up the hills into the city.

Lincoln arrived at the Palace of Machinery to the cheers of onlookers; he felt that he had waited for "Beachey Day" to arrive his whole

Three gentlemen from the Yellowstone Park exhibit at the PPIE wanted to have their picture taken with Lincoln before his second flight on March 14, 1915. Warren Eaton, with oil can in hand, has traded his usual coveralls for a business suit for Beachey Day at the Fair. *Courtesy Hud Weeks Collection*

life. Finally the whole world was acknowledging him as the greatest flyer of all time, "the Alexander of the Air"; there were even whispers of "Divine Flyer".

It was a big day for designer/mechanician Warren Eaton and brother Hillery as well, for their machine was making its first public performance. Warren had shed his usual overalls for an expensive suit, trying to be fancy for this special day, but the oil can in his hand told the full story. Lincoln checked his monoplane thoroughly, grappling with an indefinite cautiousness.

As was his custom, at three o'clock sharp Lincoln signaled Warren to spin his propeller. The motor sprang to life, Lincoln opened the throttle, and immediately he was racing along the marina green, headed for the Golden Gate. Lincoln took off, then banked out over the Bay toward Alcatraz, climbing, climbing, higher, higher. Suddenly, his motor sputtered, then sputtered again; there was obviously a bit of water

The last picture taken of Lincoln Beachey, from a newspaper clipping.

in the fuel. It would be dangerous to do much of his routine. He had enough altitude for a short program and decided to return. As he dived to gather speed for a few loops and spins on his return, he was clearly a master artist with the sky as his canvas and a new brush in his hands.

As usual, Lincoln landed to ovations, but as he got out of his machine a Fair official ran up to him and pleaded, "The traffic is so bad, the medal is not here yet, could you go up one more time?"

He could have said no, but he didn't. He wanted to check some things on his machine while Warren drained the gas tank and put in fresh fuel, but the officials interrupted him again, "Mr. Beachey, these gentlemen are from the five-acre Yellowstone replica here at the Fair and they asked if they could have their picture taken with you?"

Lincoln consented.

The fateful day, March 14, 1915, Lincoln Beachey takes off for his last flight (documented in a postcard above), powered in his new monoplane (below).

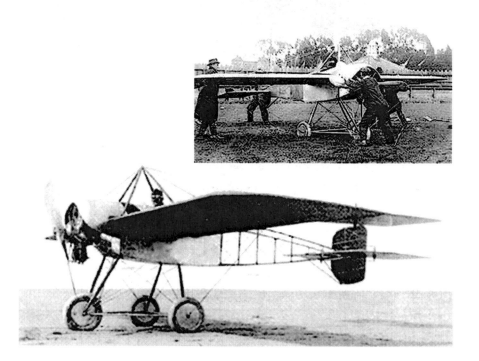

Lincoln waves goodbye as the graceful plane rises in its last flight.
Behind him, an angel waves back from the gable of one of the Fair buildings.
Close-up of Beachey's last wave. *Painting by Charles Hubbell*

Back at the plane, Eaton said to Lincoln, "I don't like the way this feels." Did Warren mean the insensitivity of the officials or something about the flight?

"I don't either, but I'm going to give them a show they'll never forget."[1]

As Lincoln climbed into his machine, a newspaper photographer flashed one last picture. At three thirty five, Beachey took off to cover for the lateness of someone else. He waved goodbye as he rose for a few minutes of show, flew out and up until he was over Angel Island, then turned back to the City. As always, he and his machine became one, like every great artist with his instrument. Lincoln felt the strength of his wings and felt they could sustain the Dive. As he passed over Alcatraz Island, he flipped his bird upside down, arched back and

The wings of the Taube, unable to withstand the stress of Lincoln's vertical dive, crumple about 500 feet above the water. *Courtesy Hud Weeks Collection*

began a long swoon downward.

Fillmore Hill and the Fair were laid out below him along old Cow Hollow. The seamlessness of the ocean and sky lay beyond the Golden Gate. Faster and faster, he plunged toward the edge of Cow Hollow but inside his cockpit Lincoln apparently could not feel the intensity and pressure that his tremendous fall was having on the wings. As he gently adjusted the controls to end the dive, his right wing failed under the severe air pressure, and broke back, then his left wing followed suit. He was now rocketing downwards at terrific speed with two broken wings.

Lincoln reached forward and turned off his motor. Then he guided the missile the Taube had become with just his rear controls to hit between two ships off the Marina. At an estimated 210 mph, Lincoln smacked into the bay waters at the edge of the Fair. Apparently he was completely relaxed, for he miraculously survived the crash. But he was thoroughly strapped into his machine, and autopsy reports remarked how he clawed at his restraints as he sank in the cold waters of San Francisco

Navy divers bring Beachey's wreckage out of the San Francisco Bay.

Bay. Lincoln Beachey drowned at the bottom of Fillmore hill.

William Randolf Hearst was watching the show with Eddie Rickenbacker and as Beachey hit the water, the newspaper giant put his arm around Beachey's fellow racer and lamented, "That's not the end of a man, but an era."

The Navy men quickly sent out trawlers, but could not snag the machine with their grappling hooks. Finally, a diver went down, and an hour and forty-five minutes after the crash the crumpled Taube was hauled to the surface with Beachey hanging from it.[2]

A gentleman in the crowd removed his hat and spoke aloud, "Hats off to Beachey." Everyone within earshot responded, and they removed their hats, and they too said, "Hats off to Beachey." And so it continued like a wave expanding out across the waters.[3]

Beachey's body was cut from the aeroplane and even though he had been underwater for an hour and forty-five minutes, resuscitation was performed for three solid hours. They couldn't believe he was dead. The San Francisco *Examiner* told the story of his passing.

A diver climbs out of a rescue boat to search the bay waters for the wreckage. This picture was made into a souvenir postcard which was sold at the Fair.

Beachey's monoplane wreckage lifted out of the water.

Beachey's body is placed in the bottom of the rowboat so that resuscitation could begin... and continued for three solid hours.

San Francisco *Examiner* documents the fatal fall.

REMOVAL OF THE BODY SUPERVISED BY MAYOR

Mayor Rolph and his young son viewed the body of Lincoln Beachey yesterday before it was taken from the morgue. Mayor Rolph said that he knew Beachey so well that he wanted to make sure that every care was exercised so that the body would have the best possible atten-

THE OMAHA DAILY

LINCOLN BEACHEY, DARE DEVIL OF AIR, KILLED IN FLIGHT

TERRIFIC FIRE OF THEIR ARTILLERY GIVES BRITISH DAY

BEACHEY KILLED IN A TAUBE DROP

Air Pressure Crumples Monoplane's Wings as Airman Tries to Resume Glide.

CROWD OF 50,000 HORRIFIED

Machine and Aeroplanist Fall Into San Francisco Bay— Recovered by Navy Diver.

BROTHER SAW HIS PLUNGE

Fatal Perpendicular Drop from 3,000 Feet Like Feat Beachey Often Had Executed in Biplane.

Special to The New York Times.

SAN FRANCISCO, March 14.—Lincoln Beachey, noted as an aviator the world over and perhaps the greatest rival of the Frenchman, Pegoud, in the execution of hair-raising aerial feats, fell to his death here today in the new German Taube monoplane in which he had been attempting to duplicate the spectacular performances of

Newspapers from around the country announce the tragedy (above).
A Navy diver searches for Beachey's body (below), and then pull him up (left). Many of the rescue effort's photos were sold as postcards since the public was deeply interested in their fallen aviator hero.

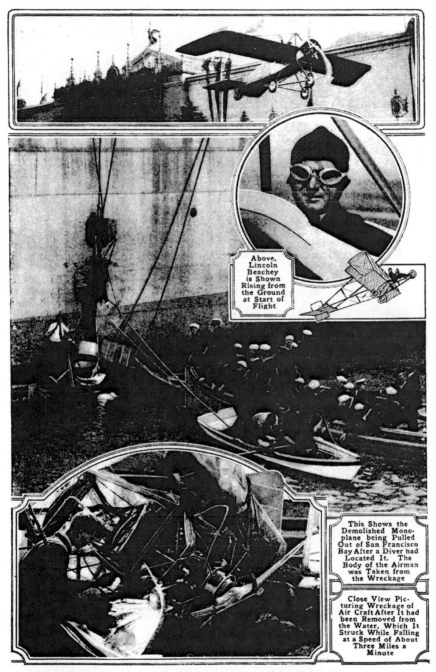

Newspaper layout honoring their fallen hero, March 14, 1915.

tion. "I wanted to personally see that his body was well taken care of and arrangements made for his funeral," the mayor said yesterday at the morgue.

FIANCÉE GIVEN NEWS BY SISTER

Beachey's tragic death tore many heartstrings. Miss Merced Walton, a strikingly beautiful young woman, Beachey's fiancée, spent the night with Beachey's mother. Denying themselves to everyone, these two women are mourning as only mother and sweetheart can the loss of one dear to both.

Miss Walton has seen Beachey fly many a time, but she was spared the sight of his fatal fall. While he was performing in the air she was directing the preparation of a dinner at the Walton home at 198 Carl Street. A merry party had been planned. Beachey was to have been there, and Mr. and Mrs. Roy A. Lee, Mrs. Lee being Miss Walton's sister, and Frank Carroll of the Goodrich Tire Company and Mrs. Carroll.

While Beachey made ready for the last flight, Miss Walton prepared for the coming of the guests. Carroll had adjusted Beachey's garment just before he was off.

The Lees and the Carrolls watched the daring young man in the air. For them the performance was nothing novel, but they knew that Beachey was fairly outdoing himself.

Meanwhile, unconscious of what was happening, Miss Walton went about her home putting the final touches on the dinner for the guests.

When the monoplane crumpled up and came down with the doomed man, Mrs. Lee, Merced Walton's sister, was first to realize that before her was a duty that was appalling.

Hurrying from the exposition grounds she went to the

Walton home, and broke the news as gently as she could.

Miss Walton was prostrated by the news. With the first outburst of grief, she realized that there was one more woman to tell—the mother.

Gathering herself, Miss Walton asked Mrs. Lee to go with her to the Fifth Avenue home. And there they found that she had already heard the news. The stricken mother and the stricken sweetheart spent the night in mourning for the boy who had gone.[4]

Three days later *The San Francisco Examiner* covered the story of Lincoln's funeral, said to be the largest in the city's history at that time. The Hearst newspaper's editorial told of the reverence the citizens of San Francisco felt for their greatest hero.

San Francisco Examiner
Monarch of the Dailies

FINAL TRIBUTE PAID TO BEACHEY BY THOUSANDS

Thousands of San Franciscans lined the streets through which the body of Lincoln Beachey was borne yesterday afternoon and stood with bowed heads in silent tribute to the young aviator.

The funeral services were conducted by the San Francisco Elks in the hall in Powell Street, and were attended by hundreds of leading citizens who were friends of Beachey.

The simple, impressive ceremony of the Elks was conducted by Lewis F. Byington, exalted ruler. The Episcopal service was read at the grave by Rev. Ernest Bradley, pastor of St. John's Church, Fifteenth and Mission Streets which Beachey attended as a boy. In the lodge-room, where the coffin rested under a blanket of pink chrysanthemums and ferns, fully 500 persons were assembled.

ENTIRE NATION MOURNS

During the course of the exalted ruler's remarks, he said the entire nation mourned the death of Lincoln Beachey. Messages of praise, sympathy and consolement had come from thousands who admired Beachey's courage, his modesty and his uprightness.

"Today," continued the speaker, "a whole city mourns. There has been no death which seemed to reach closer to the hearts of every class of our people and touch a more sympathetic cord of the man and woman of every walk of life.

"He was part of this big city, and the banker, the merchant and the man who toils in every walk of life as well as the newsboy in the street felt a clutch at his heart and a dimness in his eye when the message was flashed through the land that this brave and loyal youth had gone to his death."

ALL HEARTS TOUCHED

The words of praise brought many handkerchiefs from pockets. Mrs. Amy Beachey, the elderly, bent mother of the dead aviator, bowed her head in sorrow on the shoulder of Miss Merced Walton, the beautiful young woman whom Lincoln Beachey had asked to be his wife. Hillery Beachey, brother of the dead air pilot, seated by his mothers' side trembled with emotion and grief.

At the conclusion of the ceremony Mayor Rolph spoke a word of consolation to the bereaved mother and shook her tenderly by the hand. Those assembled then viewed the body and passed out into the street.

The funeral procession was several blocks long, extending from Elk's hall on Powell Street hill to Market

Street. It was led by a detachment of police, followed by the Elk's drill team in full regalia. Next in formation were the members of San Francisco Lodge and representatives of the Olympic Club and a company of the Sons of Veterans, all of which orders and organizations Beachey was a member. After the hearse and pallbearers came the mourners and a long line of automobiles.

At Mt. Olivet Cemetery short services were conducted and the boy's choir of St. John's Episcopal church sang a chant, "Lord, let me know mine end," and anthem, "God Shall Wipe Away All Tears" and the hymn, "Abide With Me."

The services were closed by the company from the Sons of Veterans. After a short eulogy by Commander Glen J. Sipes and M. P. Seeley, a volley was fired, the bugler sounded taps and Lincoln Beachey, world famed aviator, was laid to rest.[5]

The Bulletin

SAN FRANCISCO, WEDNESDAY, MARCH 17, 1915.

SCENE AT THE BEACHEY FUNERAL

Notes

1. San Francisco *Examiner*, March 15, 1915.   4. Ibid.

2. San Francisco *Chronicle*, March 15, 1915.   5. San Francisco *Examiner*, March 18, 1915.

3. San Francisco *Examiner*, March 15, 1915.

This picture somehow sums up Beachey's unique position as
the greatest birdman of his time, as well as his loneliness;
even the misspelling adds to the picture's poignancy.

Epilogue

News of Beachey's death flashed across the screens of movie houses everywhere, and the story of his fatal flight made headlines worldwide. Throughout the night and much of the next day, telephone operators in San Francisco received so many calls regarding the death of the nation's favorite flyer that the entire city's telephone system jammed for twenty-four hours. Beachey's death was especially shocking to the children who had watched him fly so many times since the opening of the fair, so local schools let out early the next day. Many of the older boys had gone to school wearing black armbands in honor of their fallen hero. The next afternoon, at 3:45, the minute of his death, all activity ceased on the Exposition grounds and throughout the city as fairgoers and San Franciscans observed three full minutes of silence in memory of the fallen aviator.[1]

The San Francisco board of Supervisors adopted a proposal for a memorial to Beachey, to be erected in Golden Gate Park. Mayor James Rolph was among the first to donate to the subscription.[2] The California State Senate passed a resolution honoring Beachey, and a fund was established for a memorial.[3] When the *Lusitania* was sunk by Germany not three months later (May 7, 1915), America began its shift from

Beachey's daring premonition; Beachey's mom at his grave in the '20s.

neutrality to serious involvement in the war. Plans for the monument were put on hold until after the growing world conflict in Europe was over. The money collected was later donated to the war effort as America joined her allies overseas.

With the declaration of war, the US government declared an end to the Wright-Curtiss battle and in July 1917 imposed a national pooling of aircraft patents. The patent was to be shared equally by both the Wright Company and Curtiss. Only then did US aerial development begin in earnest. A Wright-protege, Grover Loening, said the ruling would "lay the Wright patent fight into a deep grave, never to rise again." Orville continued to devote his life to aviation and served as honored adviser on numerous panels and boards.

To keep Lincoln's memory alive, Lillian Gatlin, a native San Franciscan, proposed to the city's executive committee that March 14 be set aside to pay tribute annually to the city's greatest hero. The proposal was accepted, but not until after the war did the relatively small and private commemoration become a general public ceremony.

American, French, British, and German fliers became famous as a result of their colorful and often fatal aerial battles during World War I. They extended the capabilities of aviation in their dogfighting, the military extension of Beachey's maneuvers. It is noteworthy that America's number one ace was Lincoln's friend, Eddie Rickenbaker.

After the War, on March 14, 1920, a dramatic aerial ceremony was held honoring the famous birdman. In the city's "first aeroplane parade," five flyers circled the spot above the bay where Lincoln died. Lillian Gatlin dropped pink roses, Lincoln's favorite flowers, into the waters from one of the circling planes. Below on the marina field near the still-standing Column of Progress, Colonel H.H. Arnold, the Army's air service officer for the coast, acted as master of ceremonies for the occasion. Hap Arnold was the young lieutenant who had defended Lincoln to his superior officer when Beachey flew in College Park, Maryland, in 1912. Inspired by Lincoln's flying, Arnold had dedicated himself to seeing that the military made use of the aeroplane—and went on to become the Air Force's only five star general (and commanded all Allied Air Forces over the European Theatre in WWII). Mayor Rolph and dignitaries from the Olympic and Pacific Aero Clubs addressed the crowd of ten thousand and celebrated the unsurpassed skill and bravery of their lost hero. The Pacific Aero Club announced that Beachey Day, March 14th, would be commemorated every year, to "honor not only Lincoln Beachey, but to pay tribute to all aviators who have perished in the pursuit of their hazardous calling."[4]

The next year, 1921, Beachey Day grew much larger, and many of Lincoln's earlier postcards were reissued for the commemoration. Lincoln's friend Eddie Rickenbacker, now a national war hero, came from the East Coast to join in the ceremonies and give a speech on Lincoln's remarkable character and outstanding contributions to aviation. He credited Beachey with developing the maneuvers that every ace needed to know to stay alive in a dogfight. "The aerobatics that Beachey demonstrated prior to his tragic death, served as the model for all of the strategic maneuvers used by the Army's pilots during the Great War."[6] The following year, 1922, Rickenbacker was unable to attend, but sent a fleet of his new touring cars, called the *"Rickenbackers,"* for chauffeured transportation to the ceremonies.[7]

In 1923, eight years after his death, thousands still gathered in San Francisco on Beachey Day. President Coolidge and General Pershing sent a telegrams praising Beachey's contribution to aviation and suggested that the day be given national recognition. It would be known as "Aerial Day", in honor of all fallen aviators.[8]

Finally, in 1924, the memorial planned for the fallen hero was proposed again, this time in grand style. At the time, San Francisco was the only major city on the West Coast still without a municipal airfield. The San Francisco's Flyer's Club, with the full endorsement of the Chamber of Commerce and the Downtown Association, proposed that a full scale airport be built at the Marina. This was the site where the World's Fair had taken place, on land the city already owned. The San Francisco Airport would be called THE LINCOLN BEACHEY MEMORIAL FLYING PARK, complete with a monument honoring the city's beloved flyer.[9] But because of a clause in the deed to the land which stipulated that it be forever a park, the plans for the Beachey Memorial were again postponed. The airport was moved south, near where the Tanforan Meet of 1911 had been held, but where the San Francisco Board of Supervisors recommendation no longer applied. Beachey's name fell from prominence.

As the decade progressed, the stories of World War I's heroic flying aces, the circus-like antics of barnstormers, and the trans-Atlantic flight of Charles Lindbergh eclipsed the memory of the world's greatest aviator. The Great Depression and World War II pushed the name of Lincoln Beachey even further into obscurity, and plans for his monument were never realized. Beachey Day fell from recognition, and the impact of Lincoln's achievements were largely forgotten by the American public. Still, pink roses are dropped into the Bay waters where he died every Beachey Day by fans of every generation. On the fiftieth anniversary, in 1965, Hud Weeks, a life-long Beachey fan, dropped the roses from an airplane, and on the seventy-fifth anniversary in 1990, my friends and I did the same. I continue to serve his grave.

Hillery Beachey never fully recovered from his brother's death and died in a mental hospital in southern California in 1964. Just after his death, a collection of several hundred newspapers covering the exploits of Lincoln Beachey were found in an alley in San Diego. They were turned over to the Aerospace Museum in Balboa Park in San Diego, who put them in the safe. In 1969, the museum burned to the ground and the only things saved were in the safe. In the early seventies, when the San Diego Aerospace Museum was rebuilt after the devastating fire, a repli-

Beachey's headstone has his Little Looper etched in stone.

ca of the famous Little Looper biplane was installed, surrounded by dozens of front page headlines about Beachey.

In 1966, Lincoln was inducted to the Aviation Hall of Fame in Dayton, Ohio, and in 1990, he was at last admitted to the International Aerobatics Hall of Fame, *as its founder!* That this great man in American history has been largely forgotten is almost as tragic as his death itself.

NOTES

1. Personal interviews with people who attended the Panama Pacific Exposition.
2. San Francisco *Examiner*, March 15, 1915.
3. San Francisco *Call Bulletin*, March 15, 1920
4. Hap Arnold eventually became the Air Force's only five-star general, and Supreme Commander of all allied air forces in Europe during World War II.
5. San Francisco *Examiner*, March 14, 1920
6. San Francisco *Examiner*, March 14, 1921
7. San Francisco *Examiner*, March 14, 1922
8. San Francisco Examiner, September 17, 1923
9. San Francisco Examiner, March 14, 1924

Memorial
~

Why is it that the newsies' cry
Is sad and almost stilled?
I seem to hear a sobbing sigh.
They say that Beachey&s been killed.

Our Viking of the air laid low?
That might spirit crushed?
No wonder voices tremble so,
No wonder all seems hushed.

A thousand times we&ve see you wheel
And hurtle through the sky.
A thousand times with death at your heel
You&ve carved your name star high.

Ah, Lincoln boy, your flight is done &
No more you&ll chart the blue.
You&ve played with death, and death has won,
As death must always do.

You died while on the wing, old chap,
And though we cannot know,
We fell that after all mayhap
You would have wished it so.

—George McManus, San Francisco Examiner
March 15, 1915

Lincoln Beachey
Delighting hosts unnumbered
Upward he took his flight,
As fearless as an eagle,
Far to the dizzy height.

He conquered not for glory—
He of unblemished name—
He reveled in the heavens
And modestly won fame.

While as spellbound we watched him
And stood with bated breath,
Swiftly he plunged to earthward,
Down with wings of death.

Now is his name immortal,
Now is his soul at rest.
Remember Lincoln Beachey,
Beloved still and blessed.

This King of the Air is gone
His victories are o'er,
And we shall see him soaring
Above the clouds no more.

—E. A. Sayce

A Jump-Rope Rhyme

Lincoln Beachey thought it was a dream
To go up to heaven in a flying machine.
The machine broke down and down he fell,
Instead of going to heave he went to ___.
Lincoln Beachey thought is was a dream....

—sung by San Francisco children in the 1920's

Bibliography

Aviation Quarterly, Volume Seven, Number Three, Second Quarter, 1984.

Cardin, Martin. *The Barnstormers*: Duell, Sloan & Pearce. 1965.

Cooke, Jean; Kramer, Ann, and Rowland-Entwistle, Theodore. *History's Timeline*: Crown Publishers, Inc. 1981.

Crouch, Tom. *The Bishop's Boys*: New York, W.W. Norton and Company, Inc. 1989.

Drogheda, Countess of Jane's. *Historical Aircraft, from 1902 to 1916*: Sampson, Low, Marston & Co. Ltd., 1917. Doubleday, 1972.

Dwiggins, Don. *The Air Devils*: J. P. Lippincott Co. 1966.

Harris, Sherwood. *The First to Fly, Aviation's Pioneer Days*: New York, Simon & Schuster, 1970.

Hatfield, David D.Dominguez. *Air Meet*: Northrop University Press, 1976.

Morris, Lloyd and Smith, Kendall. *Ceiling Unlimited*: New York, The Macmillan Company, 1953.

Pellegreno, Ann. *Iowa Takes To The Air*: Aerodrome Press, 1980.

Porter, Nancy, Writer & Producer. *The Wright Stuff*: The American Experience.

Prendergast, Curtis. *The First Aviators*: New York, Time Life Books, 1980

Rickenbacker, Edward V. *Eddie Rickenbacker*: Prentice-Hall 1967.

Rolt, L.T.C. *The Aeronauts*: Walker & Company, 1966.

Roseberry, C.R. *Glenn Curtiss: Pioneer of Flight*: New York, Doubleday & Co. Inc., 1972.

Scamehorn, Howard. *Balloons to Jets*: Henry Regnery Company. 1957.

Schlesinger, Arthur M. Jr., General Editor. *The Almanac of American History*: The Putnam Publishing Group, 1983.

The Blue Book: A Comprehensive Official Souvenir View Book: Robert Reid Publishing Company, 1915.

The Official Guide, The Panama Pacific International Exposition, 1915: The Wahlgreen Company, 1915.

Whitehouse, Arch. *The Early Birds*: Doubleday and Co., Inc. 1965.

THE VIEW
FROM DELPHI

Rhapsodies of Hellenic Wisdom
and
An Ecstatic Appreciation of Western History

Frank Marrero

RECOLLECTIONS
OF
SOKRATES

Frank Marrero
Evolysios

*Big Philosophy
for
Little Kids*

Writing with Character!
An Integral Curriculum of Writing Projects

Adaptable to Children in Grades 2 - 6
(with Common Core Standards Indicated)

Frank Marrero, M.A.T.

A Monkey's Tale
For the Divine Person

Leela in Praise of Beloved Adi Da Samraj

Frank Marrero

DEEP ROOTS

Illuminations in Etymology

Frank Marrero, *Evolysios*

Telling Fish about Water

On the Process of Perception
&
True Seeing

Frank Marrero
Evolysios

The
Superpowers!

of Therapeutic
Fasting

Ancient Advice and Medical Miracles

Frank Marrero, *Evolysios*
with Upton Sinclair's The Fasting Cure

Also by Frank Marrero

The View from Delphi: Rhapsodies of Hellenic Wisdom

Deep Roots: Illuminations in Etymology

Recollections of Sokrates: An Intimate View of the Sage of Athens

Songs of Deliverance: A Depository of Orphic Wisdom

The Superpowers of Fasting: Ancient Advice and Medical Miracles

Big Philosophy for Little Kids: Writing with Character!

A Monkey's Tale for the Divine Person: Leelas in Praise of Beloved Adi Da Samraj

Forthcoming:

Telling Fish About Water: On the Process of Perception and True Seeing

The Early Life Adventures of Frankie Free Boy: Naive Tales from a Most Ridiculous Life

The Anatta Upanishad: The Three Hearts and the Five Sheaths of Illusion

www.frankmarrero.com